GCSE Edexcel 360Science
Chemistry
The Workbook

This book is for anyone doing **GCSE Edexcel 360Science Chemistry**.

It's full of **tricky questions**... each one designed to make you **sweat** — because that's the only way you'll get any **better**.

There are questions to see **what facts** you know. There are questions to see how well you can **apply those facts**. And there are questions to see what you know about **how science works**.

It's also got some daft bits in to try and make the whole experience at least vaguely entertaining for you.

What CGP is all about

Our sole aim here at CGP is to produce the highest quality books — carefully written, immaculately presented and dangerously close to being funny.

Then we work our socks off to get them out to you — at the cheapest possible prices.

Contents

Published by Coordination Group Publications Ltd.

Editors:
Amy Boutal, Katherine Craig, Sarah Hilton, Kate Houghton, Kate Redmond, Ami Snelling.

Contributors:
Michael Aicken, Mike Bossart, Mike Dagless, Ian H. Davis, Max Fishel, Rebecca Harvey, Munir Kawar, Lucy Muncaster, Dr. Mark J Pilkington, Andy Rankin, Sidney Stringer Community School, Paul Warren, Chris Workman, Dee Wyatt.
From original material by Paddy Gannon.

ISBN: 978 1 84146 568 5

With thanks to Barrie Crowther, Glenn Rogers and Julie Wakeling for the proofreading.
With thanks to Katie Steele for the copyright research.

Graph on page 36 reproduced with permission of the Royal Meteorological Society.

Graphs to show trend in atmospheric CO_2 concentration and global temperature on page 38 based on data by EPICA Community Members 2004 and Siegenthaler et al 2005.

Data used to construct pie chart on page 134 from "Concise Dictionary of Chemistry" edited by Daintith, J (1986). By permission of Oxford University Press. www.oup.com

GORE-TEX®, GORE®, and designs are registered trademarks of W. L. Gore and Associates. This book contains copyrighted material reproduced with the permission of W.L. Gore and Associates. Copyright 2006 W.L. Gore and Associates.

Groovy website: www.cgpbooks.co.uk

Printed by Elanders Hindson Ltd, Newcastle upon Tyne.
Jolly bits of clipart from CorelDRAW®

Atoms

Q1 Draw a diagram of a **helium atom** in the space provided and label each type of **particle** on your diagram.

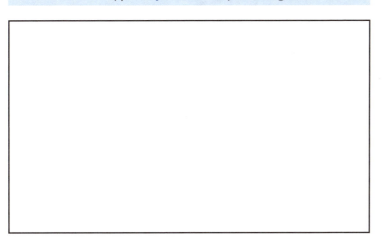

Helium has 2 of each type of particle.

Q2 **Complete** this table.

Particle	Mass	Charge
	1	+1
Neutron	1	
Electron		−1

Q3 **Complete** the following sentences by filling in the gaps or circling the correct options.

a) Neutral atoms have a charge of ....

b) A charged atom is called an ....

c) A neutral atom has the same number of .... and ....

d) If an electron is added to a neutral atom, the atom becomes **positively** / **negatively** charged.

Q4 **What is it?**

Choose from: **nucleus   proton   electron   neutron**

a) It's in the centre of the atom and contains protons and neutrons. ....

b) It moves around the nucleus in shells. ....

c) It's very light. ....

d) It's heavy and has no charge. ....

Elements

Q1 Fill in the blanks to complete the following passage about **elements** and **atoms**.

An element is a substance that is made up from only one type of ....

Atoms of different elements always contain different numbers of ....

and different numbers of electrons. The number of protons in an atom is called the

.... number. The total number of protons and neutrons in an atom is

called the .... number.

Q2 The diagrams below show four different substances. Circle those that contain only **one element**.

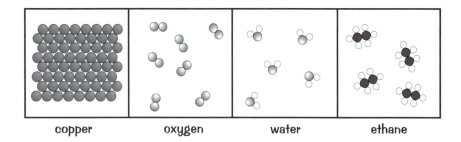

copper   oxygen   water   ethane

Q3 Many everyday substances, e.g. gold and aluminium, are **elements**.
Other substances like air and sugar are not.

Explain what this means in terms of the **atoms** in these substances.

....

....

Q4 Fill in the table below, using a periodic table to help you.

Element	Symbol	Mass Number	Number of Protons	Number of Electrons	Number of Neutrons
Sodium	Na		11		
		16	8	8	8
Neon			10	10	10
	Ca			20	20

Mixtures and Compounds

Q1 **Sea water** is a **mixture** of water and various dissolved solids, such as sodium chloride (table salt). **Water** is a **compound** of **hydrogen** and **oxygen**. Are the following statements **true** or **false**?

True False

a) All of the dissolved solids in sea water are chemically bonded to the water. ☐ ☐

b) Water can be separated into hydrogen and oxygen by boiling it. ☐ ☐

c) When all the water is evaporated off sea water, the only thing that is left is table salt. ☐ ☐

d) The formula for water is H_2O because a molecule of water has two hydrogen atoms joined to one oxygen atom. ☐ ☐

Q2 Choose from the words given to fill in the blanks in the passage below.

You may use some words more than once.

compounds   electrons   different from   elements   bonds   identical to   separate   taking

When atoms of different elements react they form bonds by giving away or sharing

.... The chemicals produced are called .... and are

usually very difficult to .... back into elements using physical methods. The

properties of compounds are .... those of the elements used to make them.

Mixtures are usually relatively easy to .... because there are no chemical

.... between their different parts.

Q3 The names of compounds can tell us what **elements** they contain.

a) Which elements are present in potassium nitrate? ....

b) Which elements are present in calcium carbonate? ....

Q4 Hassan mixes some **iron** filings and some yellow **sulphur** powder together in a beaker and leaves them overnight. The next day he holds a magnet over the beaker and the iron filings jump up and stick to it.

a) Did the iron and sulphur react to form a compound when they were left together? How can you tell?

....

b) i) Hassan tries heating the mixture. This causes the yellow solid to turn grey. Which of the following statements best describes why the yellow colour disappears? Underline your answer.

A The sulphur has evaporated.   B The sulphur has reacted with the iron.

C Sulphur changes colour when heated.   D The iron has expanded and is hiding the sulphur.

ii) Do you think that Hassan will still be able to separate the iron from the sulphur using a magnet? Explain your answer.

....

Chemical Reactions

Q1 Match these common chemical reactions to the **speed** at which they happen.

a firework exploding		a match burning
hair being dyed	SLOW (hours or longer)	
	MODERATE SPEED (minutes)	oil paint drying
an apple rotting	FAST (seconds or shorter)	

Q2 Circle the correct words to complete the sentences below about **rates of reaction**.

a) The **higher** / **lower** the temperature, the faster the rate of a reaction.

b) A **higher** / **lower** concentration will reduce the rate of a reaction.

c) A smaller particle size **increases** / **decreases** the rate of a reaction.

d) A catalyst **speeds up** / **slows down** a reaction without being used up.

Q3 Below are some descriptions of different **chemical reactions**.

A When magnesium burns in air it reacts with the oxygen present to form a white smoke of magnesium oxide.

B If magnesium carbonate is heated it decomposes to form magnesium oxide and carbon dioxide.

C A piece of potassium metal will react with water to produce potassium hydroxide and hydrogen gas. The reaction gives out enough heat to set the hydrogen gas alight.

a) List all the reactants and all the products in each case.

A Reactants: .... Products: ....

B Reactants: .... Products: ....

C Reactants: .... Products: ....

b) Which of reactions A, B and C are **endothermic**? ....

Q4 Circle the correct words to complete these paragraphs about **exothermic** and **endothermic** reactions.

a) Exothermic reactions **take in** / **give out** energy, usually in the form of **heat** / **sound**. This is often shown by a **fall** / **rise** in **temperature** / **mass**.

b) **Neutralisation** / **Decomposition** reactions are exothermic.

c) Endothermic reactions **take in** / **give out** energy, usually in the form of **heat** / **sound**. This is often shown by a **fall** / **rise** in **temperature** / **mass**.

d) **Neutralisation** / **Decomposition** reactions are endothermic.

Chemical Reactions

Q5 Limestone (**calcium carbonate**, $CaCO_3$) decomposes when it's heated to form quicklime (calcium oxide, CaO) and carbon dioxide.

There's practice on balancing equations on pages 6 and 7.

a) Write a balanced symbol equation for this reaction.

....

b) The reaction requires a large amount of heat.

   i) Is it **exothermic** or **endothermic**? ....

   ii) Explain your answer. ....

   ....

Q6 In an experiment to investigate **reaction rates**, strips of **magnesium** were put into tubes containing different concentrations of **hydrochloric acid**. The time taken for the magnesium to 'disappear' was measured. The results are shown in the table.

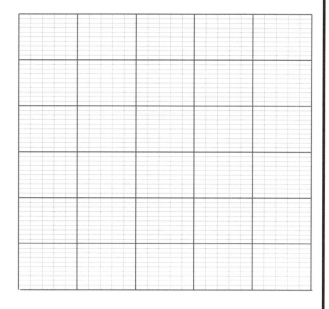

Conc. of acid (mol/dm³)	Time taken (seconds)
0.01	298
0.02	147
0.04	74
0.08	37
0.10	30
0.20	15

a) Give three things that should be kept the same in each case to make this a fair test.

....

....

b) Plot a graph of the data on the grid provided, with the concentration of the acid on the horizontal axis and the time on the vertical axis.

c) What do the results tell you about how the concentration affects the rate of the reaction?

....

d) Explain whether it would affect the rate of the reaction if magnesium powder was used instead.

....

....

Balancing Equations

Q1 Which of the following equations are **balanced** correctly?

Correctly balanced   Incorrectly balanced

a) $CuO + HCl \rightarrow CuCl_2 + H_2O$ ☐ ☐

b) $N_2 + H_2 \rightarrow NH_3$ ☐ ☐

c) $CuO + H_2 \rightarrow Cu + H_2O$ ☐ ☐

d) $CaCO_3 \rightarrow CaO \rightarrow CO_2$ ☐ ☐

e) $Al + Fe_2O_3 \rightarrow Al_2O_3 + Fe$ ☐ ☐

Q2 **Carbon monoxide** is made in fires when there is not enough oxygen available. The **unbalanced** equation is shown below:

$$C + O_2 \rightarrow CO$$

Here are three students' attempts to balance it.

Tick the box next to the correctly balanced symbol equation below.

☐ $C + O_2 \rightarrow CO_2$

☐ $C + O_2 \rightarrow 2CO$

☐ $2C + O_2 \rightarrow 2CO$

Q3 Gertrude reads in the 'Girls Own Book of Chemistry' that "**methane** (CH_4) can be burnt in **oxygen** (O_2) to make **carbon dioxide** (CO_2) and **water** (H_2O)".

a)   What are the reactants and the products in this reaction?

Reactants: ....   Products: ....

b)   Write the word equation for this reaction.

....

c)   Write the balanced symbol equation for the reaction.

....

Don't forget the oxygen ends up in both products.

Top Tips: The most important thing to remember with balancing equations is that you can't change the **little numbers** — if you do that then you'll change the substance into something completely different. Right, now that I've given you that little gem of knowledge, you can carry on with the rest.

Balancing Equations

Q4 Write out the balanced **symbol** equations for the picture equations below (some of which are unbalanced).

a)

Na Na + Cl Cl → Na Cl / Na Cl

You can draw more pictures to help you balance the unbalanced ones.

....

b)

Li + O O → Li O Li

....

c)

Mg O C O O + H Cl → Cl Mg Cl + H O H + O C O

....

d)

Li Li + H O H / H O H → Li O H + H H

....

Q5 Add **one** 'big' number to each of these equations so that they are **correctly balanced**.

a) .... CuO + ... HBr → .... $CuBr_2$ + ... H_2O

b) .... H_2 + ... Br_2 → .... HBr

c) .... Mg + ... O_2 → $2MgO$

d) $2NaOH$ + ... H_2SO_4 → .... Na_2SO_4 + ... H_2O

There are spaces in front of all the molecules — if a molecule doesn't need a number in front, just leave it blank.

Q6 **Balance** these equations.

a) .... $NaOH$ + ... $AlBr_3$ → .... $NaBr$ + ... $Al(OH)_3$

b) .... $FeCl_2$ + ... Cl_2 → .... $FeCl_3$

c) .... N_2 + ... H_2 → .... NH_3

d) .... Fe + ... O_2 → .... Fe_2O_3

e) .... NH_3 + ... O_2 → .... NO + ... H_2O

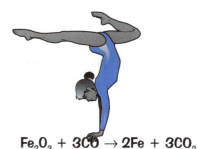

$Fe_2O_3 + 3CO \rightarrow 2Fe + 3CO_2$

A Brief History of the Periodic Table

Q1   Fill in the gaps using the words provided to complete the following passage.

properties   atomic mass   periodic   reactive

> Early versions of the periodic table listed the known elements in order of their
>
> .... When this was done it was found that ....
>
> of the elements, such as how .... they were, repeated at regular
>
> intervals. These are known as .... patterns.

Q2   Say whether the following statements about **Mendeleev's** Table of Elements are **true** or **false**.

a)   Mendeleev left gaps in the table for undiscovered elements.   ....

b)   Mendeleev arranged the elements in order of increasing atomic number.   ....

c)   Mendeleev was able to predict the properties of undiscovered elements.   ....

d)   Elements with similar properties appeared in the same rows.   ....

Q3   Mendeleev predicted the discovery of an element that would fill a gap in his Group 4, and called it '**ekasilicon**'.

The table shows the **densities** of known elements in this group.

'Ekasilicon' was eventually discovered and given another name. Use the table to decide which of the elements below is ekasilicon. Circle your choice.

Element	Density g/cm^3
carbon	2.27
silicon	2.33
ekasilicon	
tin	7.31
lead	11.3

palladium, 12.0 g/cm^3 germanium, 5.32 g/cm^3 beryllium, 1.85 g/cm^3 copper, 8.92 g/cm^3

Q4   Early forms of the periodic table were quite **different** in some ways from the modern version.

a)   Modern periodic tables list the elements in order of their atomic number.
Why didn't scientists do this when the early forms of the periodic table were created?

....

....

b)   Why don't early versions of the periodic table include Group 0 (the noble gases)?

....

c)   Which one of the following correctly explains why periodic patterns in the properties of the chemical elements were not easily observed before the 19th century? Underline your answer.

A Scientists only started looking for patterns in the world around them after 1800.

B It was hard to see patterns before the 19th century because relatively few elements were known.

C Early scientists measured the properties of elements incorrectly, so the patterns couldn't be seen.

The Periodic Table

Q1   The **periodic table** contains all the known elements.

a)   Roughly how many elements have been discovered or created so far? ....

b)   Complete the sentences below.

   i)   In the modern periodic table, the known elements are ordered according to their

   ....

   ii)   Before this, the known elements were arranged in order according to their

   ....

Q2   Choose from the words in the box to fill in the blanks in the sentences below.

left	right	horizontal	similar	different
vertical	metals	non-metals	transition	

a)   A period in the periodic table is a .... row of elements.

b)   Most of the elements in the periodic table are ....

c)   The elements between Group 2 and Group 3 are called .... metals.

d)   Non-metals are found on the .... side of the periodic table.

e)   Elements in the same group have .... properties.

Q3   Tick the correct boxes to show whether the following statements are **true** or **false**.   **True False**

a)   Elements in a group have the same number of electrons in their outer shells.   ☐ ☐

b)   The periodic table shows the elements in order of descending atomic number.   ☐ ☐

c)   Each horizontal row in the periodic table contains elements with similar properties.   ☐ ☐

d)   The periodic table includes all the known compounds.   ☐ ☐

Q4   **Argon** is an extremely unreactive gas. Use the periodic table to name two more elements that you would expect to have **similar properties** to argon.

....

Q5   Use a **periodic table** to help you answer the following questions.

a)   Name one element in the same period as silicon.   ....

b)   Name one element in the same group as potassium.   ....

c)   Name one element that is a halogen.   ....

d)   Name one element that is an alkali metal.   ....

10

Group 1 — The Alkali Metals

Q1   **Sodium**, **potassium** and **lithium** are all alkali metals.

a)   Highlight the location of the alkali metals on this periodic table.

b)   Put sodium, potassium and lithium in order of increasing reactivity.

least reactive   ....

....

most reactive   ....

c)   Explain why the alkali metals become more reactive as their atomic number increases.

....

....

Q2   Three different **alkali metals**, A, B and C, were dropped into bowls of water. The time taken for each piece to **vanish** was recorded and is shown in the table.

METAL	TIME TAKEN TO VANISH (s)
A	27
B	8
C	42

a)   i)   Why is it important that the three pieces of metal should be the same size?

....

....

ii)   Which of these is the most reactive metal? How can you tell?

....

....

iii)   The three metals used were lithium, sodium and potassium. Use the results shown in the table to match them up to the correct letters A, B and C.

A = ...

B = ...

C = ...

b)   i)   What products would be formed in a reaction between sodium and water?

....

ii)   Explain why the sodium appears to 'vanish' in this reaction.

....

....

Group 1 — The Alkali Metals

Q3 A piece of **lithium** was put into a beaker of water.

a) Write a word equation for the reaction that occurs.

....

b) Write a balanced symbol equation for the reaction that occurs.

....

c) The water was tested with universal indicator after the reaction finished.
What colour change would be observed, and why?

....

....

Q4 Circle the correct words to complete the passage below.

Sodium is a soft metal with **one** / **two** electron(s) in its outer shell. It reacts
vigorously with water, producing **sodium dioxide** / **sodium hydroxide** and
hydrogen / **oxygen** gas. When it reacts, it loses its outermost **proton** / **electron**,
forming an ion with a **positive** / **negative** charge.

Q5 Alkali metals are very **reactive** and easily form **bonds** with other atoms and molecules.

a) Describe how the structure of a lithium ion is different from that of a lithium atom.

....

b) When lithium reacts with chlorine, one electron moves from a lithium atom to a chlorine atom.
What are the charges on the lithium and chloride ions that are formed?

lithium ion: .... chloride ion: ....

c) Explain why the lithium and chloride ions join together in the reaction.

....

d) Write the formula for the compound lithium chloride.

....

Top Tips: Make sure that when it comes to your exam, you're all clued up on the alkali
metals. You need to know where they are in the periodic table, and what goes on in their reactions
with water. Make sure you know about how their reactivity changes as you go down the group too.

Group 7 — The Halogens

Q1   Highlight the location of the halogens in this periodic table.

Q2   Draw lines to match the halogens to their **descriptions** and **reactivity**.

HALOGEN	DESCRIPTION	REACTIVITY
bromine	green gas	most reactive
chlorine	grey solid	least reactive
fluorine	red-brown liquid	quite reactive
iodine	yellow gas	very reactive

Q3   Decide whether the statements about the halogens below are **true** or **false**.

True   False

a)   Chlorine gas is made up of molecules which each contain three chlorine atoms.   ☐ ☐

b)   Iodine does not have any practical uses because it is too reactive.   ☐ ☐

c)   The halogens become darker in colour as you move down the group.   ☐ ☐

d)   Their boiling points increase going down the group.   ☐ ☐

Q4   Name the **halogens** referred to by each of the following statements.

a)   This halogen gas is used to treat water because it is good at killing bacteria.

....

My friends killed just to make this — Sniff sniff...

PURE SPRING WATER

b)   The only element in Group 7 that is liquid at room temperature.

....

c)   A solution of this solid halogen can be used as an antiseptic to prevent cuts getting infected.

....

d)   A compound of this pale yellow gas is sometimes added to toothpaste to strengthen tooth enamel.

....

e)   If you heat this Group 7 solid it doesn't melt but turns straight into a gas.

....

Group 7 — The Halogens

Q5 Equal volumes of **bromine water** were added to three test tubes, each containing a different **halogen salt solution**. The results are shown in the table.

SOLUTION	RESULT
potassium chloride	no reaction
potassium bromide	no reaction
potassium iodide	reaction

a) Explain why there was no reaction when bromine water was added to potassium chloride solution.

....

....

b) Explain why there was a reaction when bromine water was added to potassium iodide solution.

....

....

c) Write a symbol equation for the reaction which took place in the potassium iodide solution when bromine water was added.

....

Q6 The word **halogen** means **something that forms salts**, so Group 7 elements are called the halogens because they often react to form salts.

a) Fill in the blanks in the following equations.

i) .... + bromine → aluminium bromide

ii) Potassium + ... → potassium iodide

iii) Magnesium + fluorine → ....

b) Write balanced symbol equations for each of the reactions in part a), using the formulae given in the box below.

Mg	Br_2	KI	Al	$AlBr_3$	K	F_2	I_2	MgF_2

i) ....

ii) ....

iii) ....

Top Tips: The examiners will expect you to know quite a bit about certain **groups** in the periodic table — the **halogens**, the **alkali metals**, the **noble gases** and the **transition metals**. Make sure you're clear on their general properties and how these change as you move down or up each group.

Group 0 — The Noble Gases

Q1   Where are the noble gases located in the periodic table?

....

Q2   Circle the correct word(s) in each pair to complete the following sentences about **noble gases**.

a)   The elements of Group 0 are all brightly coloured / colourless gases.

b)   The boiling points of the elements increase / decrease as you go down group 0.

c)   All Group 0 elements need to gain / lose / neither gain nor lose electrons to fill their outer shells.

Q3   The noble gases were **discovered** long after many of the other elements.

a)   Why did it take scientists so long to discover the noble gases?

....

b)   Explain why the noble gases are unreactive. ....

....

c)   What can be done to noble gases to make them visible?

....

Q4   Match up the names of the noble gases to their correct **properties** and **uses** below.

a)   **Neon**   has the lowest boiling point   used in electric light bulbs

b)   **Helium**   glows red when electricity is passed through it   used in airships and balloons

c)   **Argon**   glows violet when electricity is passed through it   used in nightlights and signs

Q5   Three gases are tested to try to **identify** them. The results of the tests are shown in the table below.

TEST	TEST RESULTS		
	GAS A	GAS B	GAS C
Balloon filled with the gas is released	Balloon sinks	Balloon rises	Balloon sinks
Lighted match dropped into jar of the gas	Goes out	Goes out	Burns brightly
Electric current passed through gas	Bright green-white glow	Bright yellow glow	Faint blue-green glow

a)   One of gases A, B and C is helium. Which one is it? Explain your answer.

....

b)   One of the gases is **not** a member of Group 0 of the periodic table.
      Which of the three gases do you think this is? Explain your answer.

....

Metals and Their Uses

Q1   Most **metals** that are used to make everyday objects are found in the **central section** of the periodic table.

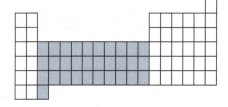

   a)   What name is given to this group of metals?

....

   b)   Give three reasons why copper is used to make electrical wires.

....

   c)   Many of the metals in this group form colourful compounds. Give two uses of this property.

....

Q2   In an experiment some identically sized rods of different materials (A, B, C and D) were **heated** at one end and **temperature sensors** were connected to their other ends. The results of the experiment are shown on the graph.

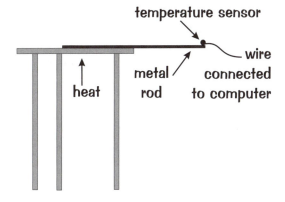
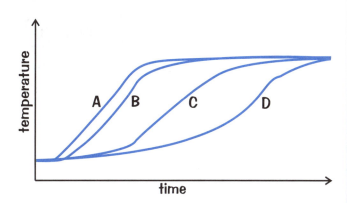

   a)   Which **two rods** do you think were made from **metals**?

....

   b)   Which of the metals was the best conductor of heat? How can you tell?

....

Q3   Imagine that a space probe has brought a sample of a new element back from Mars. Scientists think that the element is a **metal**, but they aren't certain. Give **three properties** they could look for to provide evidence that the element is a **metal**.

   1. ....

   2. ....

   3. ....

<u>Metals and Their Uses</u>

Q4 Match up the names of the following **metals** to their **properties** and **uses**.

a) **Gold**

b) **Copper**

c) **Iron**

Corrodes easily Magnetic Malleable

Doesn't corrode at all Shiny Very malleable

Doesn't corrode easily Ductile Conducts electricity very well

Electrical wiring
Water pipes

Jewellery
Shields for spacecraft

Gates and railings

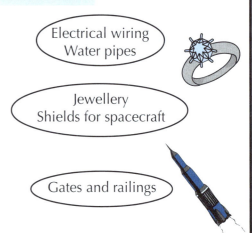

Q5 The table below lists some **properties** of two metals, **M** and **N**.

METAL	MELTING POINT (°C)	STRENGTH (MPa)	DENSITY (g/cm^3)	CORROSION RESISTANCE
M	320	100	19	excellent
N	1538	350	8	poor

a) For each of these applications, say which metal would be most suitable and justify your choice:

   i) Girders for making bridges. ....

   ii) Protective coatings for other metals. ....

   iii) Baking trays for ovens. ....

b) Which property of metal M makes it unsuitable for making lightweight frames for spectacles?

   ....

Q6 For each of the following **applications** of metals, say which **property** of the metal makes it ideal for the given use. Choose the best answer from the list of typical properties of metals below. You may only use each property **once**.

ductile   malleable   resists corrosion   conducts heat

a) Iron bars are hammered into shape to make horseshoes.   ....

b) Copper is used to make the base of saucepans and frying pans.   ....

c) Gold is used by dentists to make long-lasting fillings and false teeth.   ....

d) Copper is drawn out into thin wires for electrical cables.   ....

Identifying Compounds

Q1   **Flame tests** are often carried out to identify unknown substances.

a)   Describe how you would carry out a flame test on a sample of an unknown powder.

....

....

b)   Why would the results of this test be unreliable if the wire used had not been cleaned properly?

....

Q2   There are other tests that can be used to identify unknown metals.

a)   Describe a test (other than a flame test) that you could carry out to identify which metal is present in a compound.

....

....

b)   If this test were performed on a compound containing **copper**, what would you see?

....

Q3   Indicate whether each of the following statements is **true** or **false**.

		True	False
a)	Compounds that contain calcium produce a blue coloured flame.	☐	☐
b)	When sodium hydroxide solution is added to a solution of an iron compound, a red precipitate may form.	☐	☐
c)	When sodium hydroxide solution is added to a solution of a zinc compound, a green precipitate may form.	☐	☐

Q4   Three **metal compounds**, X, Y and Z, are tested to try and find out which metal they contain. The results of the tests are shown in the table.

a)   Identify the compound that contains these metals:

Zinc = ...

Potassium = ...

Copper = ...

Compound	Flame Colour	Colour of Precipitate formed with NaOH
X	Blue-green	Blue
Y	No visible colour	White
Z	Lilac	None formed

b)   Why is it important to perform both tests on all three compounds?

....

....

Identifying Compounds

Q5   Table salt is the compound sodium chloride together with tiny amounts of additives that help the salt flow out of its container.

a)   What could you do to provide evidence that a compound contains sodium?

....

....

....

b)   i)   If your test gives you the result that you expect, does it prove that the compound is table salt?

....

ii)   Would it be safe to put this onto food?   Explain your answer.

....

....

Q6   Burglar Bill broke into Dr Atom's chemistry lab and took a jar containing a mystery substance.   Burglar Bill was traced by the chemistry police and Dr Atom was asked to identify the substance.

Dr Atom placed some of the substance in water.   A vigorous reaction took place and the substance burnt with a lilac flame. Dr Atom was able to identify the substance from this test.

a)   What could the jar have contained?

....

b)   What group in the periodic table does this substance belong to?

....

c)   What test could Dr Atom have done to confirm his identification of the substance?

....

....

Top Tips: In your exam, you'll need to show that you'd know how to identify an unknown substance — by coming up with a suitable experiment.   You might also be given the results of an experiment and have to identify substances from the data.   It's a bit like being a detective...

C1a Topic 5 — Patterns in Properties

Chemicals in Food

Q1 Indicate whether the substances below occur **naturally** or are only made **artificially**.

Natural   Artificial

a) sodium chloride (salt)   ☐   ☐

b) tartrazine (yellow colouring)   ☐   ☐

c) glucose   ☐   ☐

d) vanillin (vanilla flavour)   ☐   ☐

e) saccharin   ☐   ☐

f) octyl ethanoate (orange flavour)   ☐   ☐

Lots of substances that occur naturally can also be made artificially. Don't worry about that — if it's found in nature, just tick 'natural'.

Wow mummy, look at that octyl ethanoate tree

Q2 Tick the correct boxes to show whether the following statements are **true** or **false**.

True   False

a) Cooking is a reversible chemical change.   ☐   ☐

b) Some artificial food additives have been linked to health problems.   ☐   ☐

c) Salt is a natural food additive which has been linked to high blood pressure.   ☐   ☐

d) Cooked potatoes contain different chemicals from raw potatoes.   ☐   ☐

e) Aspartame is a natural sweetener.   ☐   ☐

Q3 Natural vanilla contains the chemical **vanillin**.
Vanillin is also made artificially for use in ice cream.

a) What is responsible for the difference in flavour between natural vanilla and that in ice cream?

....

....

b) Some artificial flavours, e.g. artificial sweeteners, have a similar flavour to natural substances but a different chemical structure.

i) Give an example of an artificial sweetener with a different structure from sugar.

....

ii) Explain why this difference in chemical structure is an advantage.

....

....

Chemicals in Food

Q4 Explain how **cooking** helps:

a) humans to digest potatoes ....

....

b) make meat more appealing ....

....

Q5 **Health problems** have been linked to both artificial and natural **additives**.

a) Give an example of a health problem associated with each type of additive.

i) artificial ....

ii) natural ....

b) The table shows the results of some research into the effect of food additive X on the incidence of migraines. A group of 100 men and 100 women took a small dose of substance X everyday. A control group of 200 people was also monitored.

| | % suffering one or more migraines | |
	Group taking X	Control
Males	11	4
Females	4	5

i) Explain why a control group is needed.

....

ii) Describe the conditions that would be used in the control group.

....

iii) Explain why the reliability of the results would increase if the experiment was repeated by other researchers.

....

....

iv) What does the research show for the male and for the female groups?

....

....

v) In such research, **a correlation or link does not imply a cause**. Explain what this means.

....

....

Top Tips: The important thing to remember here is that there's nothing special about 'natural' compounds — they can all be copied if you can manage to stick the right atoms together in the right way.

Acids and Bases and Neutralisation

Q1   Complete the following sentences with a single word.

a)   Solutions which are not acidic or alkaline are said to be ....

b)   When a substance is neutral it has a pH of ....

c)   Indigestion occurs because the stomach produces too much .... acid.

d)   Ammonia is used to make .... like ammonium nitrate.

Q2   Draw lines to match the substances below to their **universal indicator colour**, **pH** value and **acid/base strength**.

SUBSTANCE	UNIVERSAL INDICATOR COLOUR	PH	ACID/BASE STRENGTH
a) distilled water	purple	5/6	strong alkali
b) rainwater	yellow	8/9	weak alkali
c) caustic soda	dark green/blue	14	weak acid
d) washing-up liquid	red	7	neutral
e) car battery acid	pale green	1	strong acid

Q3   Acids and bases have many different **uses**. For each of the uses given below, choose the correct acid or base from the box.

ethanoic acid	ammonia	phosphoric acid
hydrochloric acid	sodium hydroxide	citric acid

a)   Acid used in the production of petrol, nylon and detergents.   ....

b)   Base used to manufacture nitric acid and sodium carbonate.   ....

c)   Acid used as a food additive to give foods a sour taste.   ....

d)   Base used to make bleach and in soap manufacture.   ....

e)   Acid that is diluted and used as a descaling agent.   ....

f)   Acid used to manufacture PVC and to process steel.   ....

Acids and Bases and Neutralisation

Q4   Antacid tablets contain alkalis to neutralise the excess stomach acid that causes indigestion.

Joey wanted to test whether some antacid tablets really did neutralise acid. He added a tablet to some hydrochloric acid, stirred it and tested its pH. Further tests were carried out after adding a second, third and fourth tablet. His results are shown in the table below.

TABLETS ADDED	PH OF THE ACID
0	1
1	2
2	3
3	7
4	7

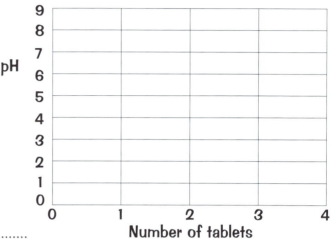

a)   **i)**   Plot a graph of the results.

ii)   Describe how the pH changes when the tablets are added to the acid.

....

....

iii)   How do the results show that the tablets reduce acidity?

....

iv)   How many tablets were needed to neutralise the acid?

....

b)   Joey tested another brand of tablets to see whether they were better at removing acidity. He found that only **two** tablets were required to neutralise the acid.

Make a sketch on the graph of the results you might expect for these tablets.

Q5   Julie wanted to make **ammonium nitrate** and use it as a **fertiliser**. She decided to make the ammonium nitrate by adding **ammonia** solution to an **acid** until it was just neutralised.

a)   Complete the general equation for the reaction between an acid and a base.

ACID + BASE → .... + ...

b)   Ammonia is a soluble base. What name is given to a soluble base? ....

c)   Which acid would be used to make ammonium nitrate? Give the word equation for the reaction.

Water isn't formed in acid/base reactions involving ammonia.

.... + ... → ....

d)   Apart from fertilisers, describe one other use of salts.

....

....

Reactions of Acids

Q1   Give the **general word equations** for the reaction between an **acid** and:

a) a **metal carbonate** ....

b) a **metal hydroxide** ....

Q2   Complete the word equations for **acids** reacting with **metal oxides**.

a) sulphuric acid + zinc oxide → .... + ...

b) hydrochloric acid + ... oxide → nickel .... + ...

Q3   Complete the following symbol equations for **acids** reacting with **metal carbonates**.

a) $2HNO_3 + Na_2CO_3 →$ .... + ... + ...

b) .... + ... $→ MgSO_4 +$ .... + ...

Q4   Amir wanted to investigate a way of restoring a tarnished copper ornament. He obtained some **copper compounds** and looked at the effect of reacting them with dilute **hydrochloric acid** (HCl).

SUBSTANCE TESTED	FORMULA	COLOUR	OBSERVATIONS WHEN ADDED TO THE ACID
copper carbonate	$CuCO_3$	green	fizzed and dissolved forming a blue solution
copper hydroxide	$Cu(OH)_2$	blue	dissolved slowly forming a blue solution
copper oxide	CuO	black	dissolved very slowly forming a blue solution

a) **i)** Why does copper carbonate fizz when it reacts with an acid?

....

     ii) Write a word equation for the reaction.

....

b) Why is the same blue solution formed with each compound?

....

c) Amir tested part of the copper ornament with the acid and it fizzed.

     i) Which compound is likely to be present on the surface of the ornament?

....

     ii) What further evidence would support this?

....

d) Write a balanced symbol equation for the reaction of hydrochloric acid with copper hydroxide.

....

Preparing Salts and Hazard Symbols

Q1 The **solubility** of some salts in **water** is shown in the table.

Salt	Solubility	Salt	Solubility
copper nitrate	soluble	calcium chloride	soluble
lead nitrate	soluble	calcium sulphate	insoluble
sodium carbonate	soluble	lead sulphate	insoluble
copper carbonate	insoluble	sodium sulphate	soluble

a) Write word equations for the formation of each insoluble salt using compounds from the table.

1. ....

2. ....

3. ....

b) What is this type of reaction called? ....

Q2 **Silver chloride** is an insoluble salt which can be made by **mixing** silver nitrate and sodium chloride solutions together.

a) Complete the symbol equation for the reaction.

$AgNO_3$(aq) + NaCl(aq) → ....(s) + ...(aq)

b) What do the two state symbols mean?

i) (aq) ....   **ii)** (s) ....

c) After mixing the solutions to produce a precipitate, what further steps are needed to produce a pure, dry sample of silver chloride?

....

....

Q3 Draw lines to match the **symbols** below with their **meanings** and **hazards**.

a) **toxic**   *can cause death if swallowed, inhaled or absorbed through the skin*

b) **corrosive**   *causes reddening or blistering of the skin*

c) **irritant**   *attacks and destroys living tissue*

Q4 **Potassium chlorate**, $KClO_3$, has this **hazard symbol** on its container:

a) Explain what the symbol means and briefly describe why $KClO_3$ is dangerous.

....

b) Potassium chlorate is one of the chemicals used in match heads. Describe its function.

....

c) Explain why potassium chlorate is stored separately from flammable or combustible materials.

....

Hydration and Thermal Decomposition

Q1 Answer the following questions about reactions involving **water**.

a) Which reaction(s) involve **dehydration**? Circle one or more letters.

   A $Cu(OH)_2(s) \rightarrow CuO(s) + H_2O(l)$

   B $C_2H_4(g) + H_2O(l) \rightarrow C_2H_5OH(l)$

   C $NiCO_3(s) \rightarrow NiO(s) + CO_2(g)$

b) Which reaction(s) involve **hydration**? Circle one or more letters.

   A $CuSO_4.5H_2O(s) \rightarrow CuSO_4(s) + 5H_2O(l)$

   B $CaO(s) + H_2O(l) \rightarrow Ca(OH)_2(s)$

   C $CH_4(g) + 2O_2(g) \rightarrow CO_2(g) + 2H_2O(g)$

   D $C_6H_{12}O_6(s) \rightarrow 6C(s) + 6H_2O(l)$

Q2 Indicate whether the following statements are **true** or **false**.

		True	False
a)	Calcium carbonate gives off carbon dioxide and water when it decomposes.	☐	☐
b)	Thermal decomposition involves breaking a substance down into simpler substances.	☐	☐
c)	Baking powder produces carbon dioxide when heated, which makes cakes rise.	☐	☐
d)	Dehydration reactions are a type of condensation reaction.	☐	☐
e)	Sugar can be hydrated by adding it to concentrated sulphuric acid.	☐	☐
f)	The dehydration of sugar gives carbon and water as its products.	☐	☐

Q3 When **hydrated copper sulphate** (blue crystals) is heated it turns into **anhydrous copper sulphate** (white powder) and **water**.

$$CuSO_4.5H_2O(s) \rightarrow CuSO_4(s) + 5H_2O(l)$$

a) Why is the reaction described as dehydration?

....

b) Why can the reaction also be described as thermal decomposition?

....

c) Why is the reverse reaction described as hydration?

....

d) Explain how the reverse reaction can be used as a simple test for water.

....

<u>*Hydration and Thermal Decomposition*</u>

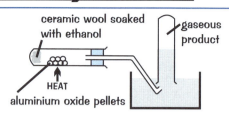

ceramic wool soaked with ethanol

gaseous product

HEAT

aluminium oxide pellets

Q4 **Ethanol** vapour is passed over hot **aluminium oxide**. The ethanol **decomposes** according to the equation:

$$C_2H_5OH \ (g) \xrightarrow{\text{heat }/Al_2O_3} C_2H_4 \ (g) \ + \ H_2O \ (g)$$

a) The ethanol decomposes during this reaction. Explain what **thermal decomposition** means.

....

b) What role does the aluminium oxide play in the reaction?

....

c) Explain how you could modify the apparatus to collect the water produced instead of the C_2H_4 gas.

....

Q5 Sam wanted to test whether **baking soda** really does **decompose** and give off gases when heated.

Experiment 1: Sam put some baking soda on a tin lid and placed it in an oven at 220 °C. After 20 minutes there appeared to be no change to the white powder.

a) Why do you think there was no apparent change?

....

(Assume that some of the baking soda decomposed.)

b) Explain fully what she could have done to show that decomposition had occurred.

....

....

c) The chemical name for baking soda is sodium hydrogencarbonate. Write a word equation for the thermal decomposition of sodium hydrogencarbonate.

....

Experiment 2: Sam used the apparatus shown to try and prove that carbon dioxide was formed when the baking soda was heated.

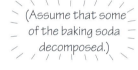

baking soda

liquid A

heat

d) i) Name liquid A and say what it is used for.

....

ii) Describe the change that should occur in liquid A during the reaction.

....

e) When you mix baking soda with an acid called cream of tartar, you get baking powder. Explain how baking powder makes cakes rise.

....

....

Metal Ores

Q1   Indicate whether each of the statements below about **metal ores** is true or false.

True **False**

a)   Ores are metal compounds that contain enough metal to make extraction worthwhile. ☐ ☐

b)   The more reactive the metal, the easier it is to extract from its ore. ☐ ☐

c)   Zinc, iron and tin can all be extracted by heating their ores with carbon monoxide. ☐ ☐

Q2   Copper may have been formed when someone accidentally dropped some copper ore into a **wood fire**. When the ashes were cleared away some copper was left.

a)   Explain how dropping the ore into the fire led to the extraction of copper.

....

b)   Why do you think that copper was one of the first metals to be extracted from its ore?

....

Q3   Fill in the blanks in the passage below.

.... can be used to extract metals that are

.... it in the reactivity series. Oxygen is removed

from the metal oxide in a process called ....

Other metals have to be extracted using ....

because they are .... reactive.

Q4   Some metals are found as **ores**. Others, such as gold, are usually found as **elements**.

a)   Explain why gold is usually found as an element.

....

b)   i) One type of iron ore is magnetite (Fe_3O_4).
Write a balanced symbol equation for its formation from iron (Fe) and oxygen (O_2).

....

   ii) Is the iron **oxidised** or **reduced** in this reaction? ....

c)   i) Write a balanced symbol equation to show the reaction that happens when aluminium is extracted from its ore, Al_2O_3.

....

   ii) Is the aluminium **oxidised** or **reduced** in this reaction? ....

Gas Tests

Q1 Which piece(s) of apparatus shown could be used to collect:

 **A** 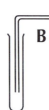 **B**  **C** 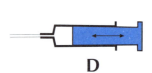 **D**

a) a gas by downward delivery? ....

b) a sample of dry ammonia gas? ....

c) a gas by upward delivery? ....

d) a specific volume of carbon dioxide given off in a reaction? ....

e) a soluble gas and monitor the rate at which it is produced? ....

Carbon dioxide is only slightly soluble in water.

Q2 A number of **gases** were collected and **tested**.

Which gas:

a) bleached damp litmus paper? ....

b) gave a 'pop' when tested with a burning splint? ....

c) turned damp red litmus paper blue? ....

d) relit a glowing splint? ....

Q3 When copper carbonate is heated it gives off **carbon dioxide**.

a) Complete the diagram to show how you could collect a test tube of the gas by **downward delivery**.

b) Why is downward delivery a suitable collection method for carbon dioxide?

....

....

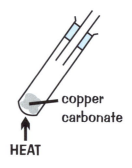
copper carbonate

HEAT

c) If potassium chlorate (KClO$_3$) is heated, a gas is produced that can be collected. Jenny thought that chlorine or oxygen might be given off.

How would she test to see which gas is given off?

....

....

Gas Tests

Q4 A flask of **dry ammonia** was collected using the apparatus shown.

a) Explain why ammonia is suitable for collection by upward delivery.

   ....

b) Damp litmus paper is used to test the gas when the flask is full.
   What colour litmus paper would be used and what colour
   change would occur when the flask is full of ammonia?

   ....

   ....

test with litmus paper
dry ammonia gas
potassium hydroxide pellets
concentrated ammonia solution
HEAT GENTLY

Q5 Jamie wanted to produce a gas jar full of **hydrogen** for an experiment.
   He knew that **zinc** could be reacted with **sulphuric acid** to produce the gas.

a) Why is it difficult to know when the gas jar is full?

   ....

b) Describe how Jamie could collect a full gas jar of hydrogen and draw a labelled diagram of the
   apparatus he should use, showing how more acid could be added during the reaction.

   ....

   ....

   ....

   ....

   ....

   ....

c) Why might more acid be needed during the experiment?

   ....

   ....

d) Write a word equation for the reaction that takes place.

   ....

e) Explain how Jamie could test the gas produced to make sure that it was hydrogen.

   ....

Top Tips: Remember the collection method depends on how dense the gas is. If it's 'lighter than air', upward delivery should be used. If it's 'heavier than air', it's downward delivery you need.

Mixed Questions — C1a Topics 5 & 6

Q1 This question concerns **substances A** to **I** below.

A F_2 (fluorine)	**B** NaCl (sodium chloride)	**C** $CuSO_4$ (copper sulphate)
D N_2 (nitrogen)	**E** CO_2 (carbon dioxide)	**F** S (sulphur)
G Na (sodium)	**H** C (graphite)	**I** MgO (magnesium oxide)

a) **i)** Which of the substances A to I are present in air?

....

ii) Explain whether the forces between the molecules in air are strong or weak.

....

b) **i)** Which substance is often used as a natural food additive? ....

ii) Give one health problem that has been linked to this natural food additive.

....

c) Substance C is harmful. Draw the hazard symbol you
would expect to see on the bottle of substance C.

Q2 The following questions relate to the **periodic table** shown below.

a) Give the symbol for the element in each of the following questions.

i) Identify an element with the same number of outer shell electrons as Se. ....

ii) Which element has the same number of electron shells as Mg? ....

iii) Identify an element that would react vigorously with water to give H_2 gas. ....

iv) Which element is a green gas that displaces bromine from KBr solution? ....

v) Identify an inert element that is used in electrical discharge tubes. ....

b) Explain, in terms of electron arrangement, which element shown in Group 1 is the most reactive.

....

....

Mixed Questions — C1a Topics 5 & 6

Q3 Below are two different reactions involving **acids**.

Acid + **X** → salt + water + carbon dioxide   Acid + **Y** → salt + water

a) Which substance, X or Y: **i)** is a metal oxide? .... **ii)** is a metal carbonate? ....

b) Both these reactions give out heat. What name is given to this type of reaction? ....

c) Another equation of an acid reaction is shown below. Balance the equation.

.... HCl + ... Na_2CO_3 → .... $NaCl$ + ... H_2O + ... CO_2

Q4 Look at the different types of **reaction** listed, and decide which type each statement refers to.

    thermal decomposition   **hydration**   **dehydration**   **precipitation**

a) Used to prepare an insoluble salt from two soluble salts. ....

b) Always endothermic. ....

c) Always has water as a product. ....

d) Always has water as a reactant. ....

Q5 **Transition metals**, found in the centre of the periodic table, are typical metals.

a) Give three properties of transition metals that make them useful.

....

b) **Iron** is extracted from its ore by heating it with carbon monoxide. **Aluminium** is extracted from its ore using electrolysis. **Gold** is usually found by itself in nature.

Put these metals in order of reactivity, beginning with the least reactive.

....

Q6 Jamal is investigating an unknown **metal carbonate**.

a) **i)** When he puts the sample in a Bunsen flame a brick red colour is seen. Which metal is present?

....

ii) Write the word equation for the reaction that occurs when the metal carbonate is heated.

....

b) **i)** Write a balanced symbol equation for the reaction between the metal carbonate and HCl.

....

ii) Explain how Jamal could collect and test for the gas produced.

....

Useful Products from Air and Salt

Q1 Answer the following questions about the **fractional distillation** of **air**.

a) Circle the correct word(s) to complete the passage below.

Air is a **compound** / **mixture** consisting of 78% **nitrogen** / **carbon dioxide** / **oxygen** and 21% **water** / **oxygen** / **nitrogen**. The other **5%** / **99%** / **1%** is mainly argon. Air also contains a small amount of **oxygen** / **carbon dioxide** and varying amounts of **water** / **nitrogen**.

b) **i)** The gases in air can be separated using **fractional distillation**. Explain why this method works.

....

ii) The first part of the distillation process is to repeatedly compress and expand the air. What is the purpose of this part of the process?

....

iii) Air liquefies at about –200 °C. The boiling points of nitrogen and oxygen are –196 °C and –187 °C respectively. If the liquefied air is slowly warmed, which gas will boil first and why?

....

Q2 Oxygen and nitrogen are both used in **industry** and in other areas.

a) Give two uses for oxygen.

....

b) Give two uses for liquid nitrogen.

....

Q3 Salt, **sodium chloride**, has many uses.

a) Describe and explain how salt is obtained on a large scale in hot countries.

....

b) What is rock salt? ....

....

c) Where did the layers of underground rock salt in Britain come from?

....

d) Explain what happens when rock salt is used on icy roads.

....

e) Refined salt is often added to processed food. Explain why, and give one disadvantage of this.

....

Useful Products from Air and Salt

Q4 The **hydrogen** produced by the electrolysis of **NaCl solution** is used in many different ways.

a) What is made using hydrogen in the Haber process? ....

b) In what ways is hydrogen used in the metal-working industry?

....

Q5 'Harry's Brine Products' is a company that **electrolyses brine** and sells the products for use in various **industries**. Harry keeps a record of the different amounts sold to the different industries, as shown in the pie chart.

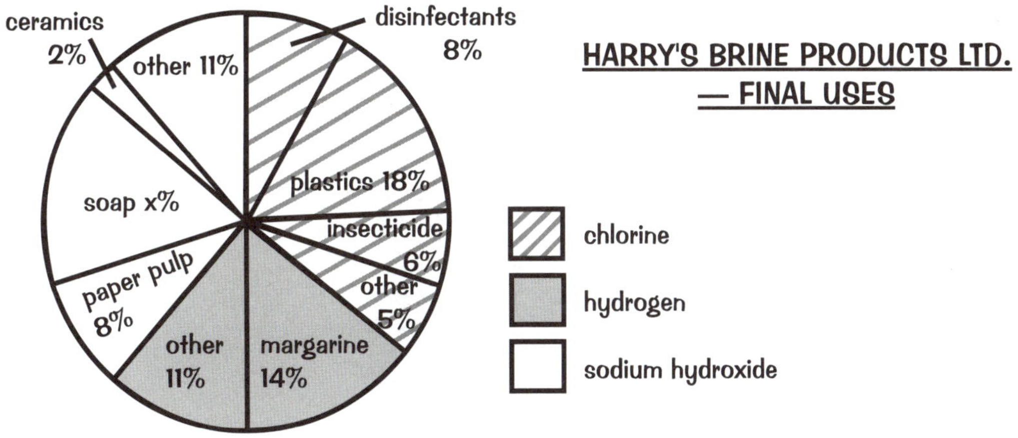

HARRY'S BRINE PRODUCTS LTD.
— FINAL USES

ceramics 2%
other 11%
disinfectants 8%
plastics 18%
soap x%
insecticide 6%
other 5%
paper pulp 8%
other 11%
margarine 14%

chlorine
hydrogen
sodium hydroxide

a) Which brine product, **hydrogen**, **chlorine** or **sodium hydroxide**, did Harry sell the most of?

....

b) What percentage of Harry's products are used to manufacture soap?

....

c) Suggest one other use of sodium hydroxide that is not mentioned on the chart above.

....

d) Which industry uses Harry's products the most?

....

e) Sodium is not one of the products of the electrolysis of brine.
Explain how sodium can be extracted from salt, and give two of its uses.

....

....

Top Tips: Remember, **electrolysis** simply means **splitting with electricity**. It's not only used to electrolyse brine but also to separate loads of metals from their ores, e.g. **aluminium**.

Fractional Distillation of Crude Oil

Q1 Circle the correct words to complete these sentences.

a) Crude oil is a **mixture** / **compound** of different molecules.

b) The molecules in crude oil **are** / **aren't** chemically bonded to each other.

c) If crude oil was heated the **first** / **last** thing to boil off would be lubricating oil.

d) Diesel has **bigger** / **smaller** molecules than petrol.

Q2 Label this diagram of a **fractionating column** to show where these substances can be collected.

diesel   kerosene   bitumen   heating oil   petrol

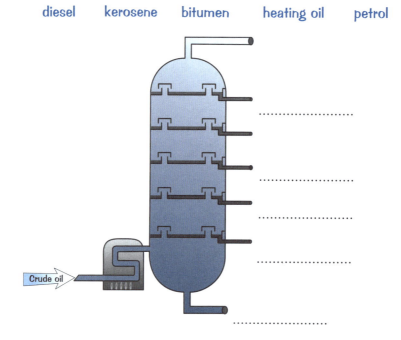

....

....

....

....

Crude oil

....

Q3 Different **fractions** obtained from crude oil have different **uses**. Match the fractions to their uses.

LPG	starting material in chemical industry
petrol	fuel for non-petrol engines in cars, trucks, trains
naphtha	car fuel
kerosene	road surfacing, roofing asphalt
diesel	bottled gas, pottery and glass-making
oil	jet fuel, paint solvent
bitumen	domestic central heating

phwoar... nice
tank, love

Q4 There are some basic **trends** in the way that hydrocarbons behave. Circle the correct words to complete these sentences.

a) The longer the alkane molecule, the **more** / **less** viscous the substance is.

b) A very volatile liquid is one with a **low** / **high** boiling point.

c) The shorter the alkane molecule, the **more** / **less** volatile the substance is.

Using Hydrocarbons

Q1   Answer the following questions about **burning hydrocarbons**.

a)   Write a **word equation** for burning a hydrocarbon in the open air.

....

b)   Write **balanced symbol equations** for burning these alkanes in the open air:

i)   Methane ....

ii) Propane ....

Q2   When choosing fuels there are a number of **factors** which must be taken into consideration. Give three factors that are important when choosing a fuel to be used in a car engine.

1. ....

2. ....

3. ....

Q3   Answer the following questions about **hydrocarbons**.

a)   Which two elements are hydrocarbons made up of? ....

b)   Underline the two correct formulae for the products of the complete combustion of a hydrocarbon.

H_2S CH_4 CO_2 SO_2 H_2O

c)   Suggest why might a fuel not burn completely?

....

....

My favourite few L's

Q4   **Incomplete combustion** can cause problems.

a)   Fill in the blanks to complete the symbol equation for the incomplete combustion of butane.

C_4H_{10} + ... → ...... H_2O + ... CO_2 + ... + ...

b)   Why is incomplete combustion:

i)   dangerous? ....

ii) a waste of fuel? ....

iii) messy? ....

Hydrocarbons and the Environment

Q1 When fossil fuels are burned they release **carbon dioxide**, **sulphur dioxide** and **nitrogen oxides**.

a) How is sulphur dioxide (SO_2) produced?

....

b) How are nitrogen oxides (NO_x) produced?

....

c) Name the acid each gas produces when it mixes with clouds in the atmosphere.

i) SO_2 makes .... **ii)** NO_x makes ....

d) Give the two main **sources** of SO_2 and NO_x.

....

Q2 **Smog** is a mixture of smoke and fog, and can be deadly.

a) Circle the correct word of each pair in the following sentence:

When **heat / sunlight** acts on **NO_x / SO_2**, photochemical smog is produced.

b) **i)** Sometimes ground-level ozone is produced. The formula for ozone is: **O_2** **O_3** **O**

ii) Give one medical problem that ozone can cause. ....

Q3 The graph shows the number of **deaths** each day in London in the first half of December 1952, against the concentration of **smoke** in mg/m³.

a) What was the highest number of deaths recorded in one day? ....

b) A student said: "The graph shows that more smoke in the air causes more deaths". Comment on this conclusion.

....

....

....

The 1952 London Smog

Q4 **Exhaust** fumes from cars and lorries often contain **carbon monoxide**.

a) Why is carbon monoxide more likely to be formed in **engines** than if the fuel was burnt in the open air?

....

b) Why is carbon monoxide **dangerous**?

....

The Evolution of the Atmosphere

Q1   Tick the boxes next to the sentences below that are **true**.

a) When the Earth was formed, its surface was molten.   ☐

b) The Earth's early atmosphere is thought to have been mostly oxygen.   ☐

c) Oxygen eventually began to build up in the Earth's atmosphere, mostly due to its release from volcanoes.   ☐

d) When some organisms died and were buried under layers of sediment, the carbon they had contained became locked up as fossil fuels.   ☐

e) The development of the ozone layer meant the Earth's temperature became suitable for complex organisms to evolve.   ☐

Q2   The pie chart on the right shows the proportions of different **gases** in the Earth's atmosphere **today**.

a) Add the labels **Nitrogen**, **Oxygen**, and **CO$_2$ & other gases**.

b) Give the approximate percentages of the following gases in the air today:

Nitrogen ....   Oxygen ....

Water vapour

c) The second pie chart shows the proportions of different gases that we think were in the Earth's atmosphere 4500 million years ago.

Describe the main differences between today's atmosphere and the atmosphere 4500 million years ago.

....

....

....

Carbon dioxide

Nitrogen

Other gases

Water vapour

d) Explain why the amount of water vapour has decreased.   *What did the water vapour turn into?*

....

e) Explain how oxygen was introduced into the atmosphere.

....

f) Describe two effects of the oxygen levels in the atmosphere rising.

1. ....

....

2. ....

....

The Evolution of the Atmosphere

Q3 Draw lines to put the statements in the **right order** on the timeline. One has been done for you.

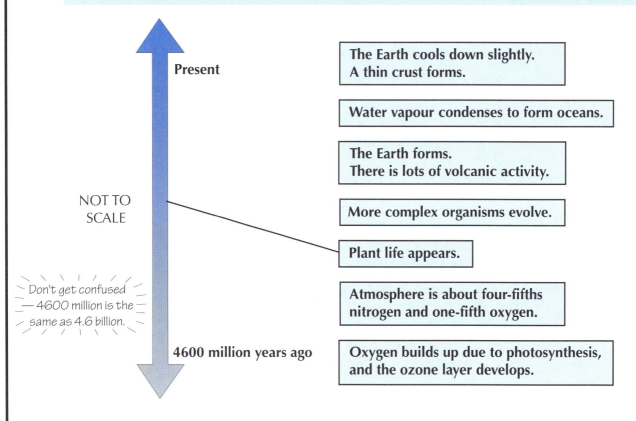

Present

NOT TO
SCALE

Don't get confused — 4600 million is the same as 4.6 billion.

4600 million years ago

The Earth cools down slightly.
A thin crust forms.

Water vapour condenses to form oceans.

The Earth forms.
There is lots of volcanic activity.

More complex organisms evolve.

Plant life appears.

Atmosphere is about four-fifths
nitrogen and one-fifth oxygen.

Oxygen builds up due to photosynthesis,
and the ozone layer develops.

Q4 The graph shows data on **global temperature** and
concentration of atmospheric CO_2 against time.

a) Suggest why the CO_2 line begins to rise rapidly
after about 1850.

....

....

....

Think about the changes in industry
that occurred around this time

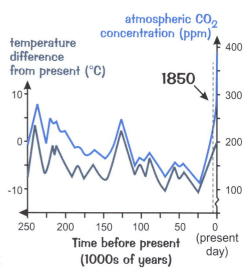

b) Mark an X on the temperature line to show when the most
recent ice age could have occurred.

c) Does **this graph** provide evidence to support the theory that global warming is a direct result of
human activity? Explain your answer.

....

....

Top Tips: So, in its early days the Earth's atmosphere was pretty **different** — loads of CO_2 and
not a lot of oxygen. Then good old **plants** came along and sorted everything out ready for the rest of us.

Climate Change

Q1 Circle the correct words of each pair to complete the passage below.

> Many scientists think that the use of **fossil** / **nuclear** fuels is linked to **a decrease** /
> **an increase** in the world's temperature. This is because when these fuels are burned,
> they give off **ozone** / **CO_2**, which is a **greenhouse** / **radioactive** gas.

Q2 **Carbon dioxide** and **methane** are two atmospheric gases which
are important in the regulation of the Earth's **temperature**.

a) Which of A, B, C and D best explains how CO_2 and methane help regulate the Earth's
temperature?

  A **They absorb heat from the Sun.** B **They keep the polar ice caps from melting.**

  C **They absorb heat from the Earth.** D **They counteract acid rain.**

b) Explain how you add to carbon dioxide production if:

  i) you are driven to school in a car instead of walking or taking the bus.

  ....

  ii) you leave the TV on standby all night.

  ....

c) Give one significant source of **methane**.

  ....

Q3 The diagram shows **radiation** from the Sun
entering the Earth's **atmosphere**.

a) Complete the diagram by showing the path
of the radiation after it enters the atmosphere.

b) What difference would it make if there was no
CO_2 or methane in the Earth's atmosphere?

  ....

  ....

  ....

  ....

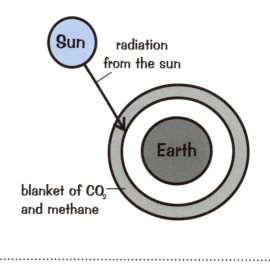

Climate Change

Q4 Scientists try to **predict** what the Earth's **temperature** will be in the future. There are various steps involved in doing this.

a) Describe briefly how monitoring stations and computers are involved in making these predictions.

....

....

b) Explain why these predictions may not be accurate.

....

....

c) How can the predictions be tested?

....

....

Q5 At the time of writing, 164 countries have ratified the **Kyoto Protocol**, an agreement to reduce CO_2, methane and other greenhouse gas emissions by an average of **5%** (compared to 1990 levels) by **2012**. Achieving this reduction will involve **changes** to the way fossil fuels are used.

a) Give two ways that countries could reduce the amount of fossil fuels they burn.

....

....

b) Rainforests once covered about 14% of the Earth's surface. They now cover about 6%. Explain briefly what impact this may have had on global warming.

....

....

Q6 The idea that global warming may be caused by rising CO_2 levels is not a new one — it was first proposed in the 1890s. Since then, a lot more evidence has become available and the majority of scientists now accept that the Earth is **gradually warming**.

a) Explain why it is hard to be 100% sure that Earth is warming and humans are to blame.

....

....

b) Give two basic strategies for combating climate change, based on the 'precautionary principle'.

....

....

Recycling

Q1 Explain what is meant by **sustainable development**.

....

....

Q2 Give three advantages of **recycling** materials such as **metals**, **paper** and **glass**.

1. ....

2. ....

3. ....

Q3 Tick the correct boxes to show whether the following statements are **true** or **false**.

		True	False
a)	Recycling could help to prevent further increases in greenhouse gas levels.	☐	☐
b)	It is important to recycle paper because there is a finite amount available.	☐	☐
c)	Recycling costs nothing and has huge benefits for the environment.	☐	☐

Q4 Below is some information about **aluminium**, a widely used metal today.

- Bauxite (aluminium ore) gives 1 kg of aluminium for every 4 kg of bauxite mined.
- Bauxite mines are often located in rainforests.
- Extracting aluminium from bauxite requires huge quantities of electricity.
- An aluminium can weighs about 20 g.

a) **i)** How much ore has to be mined to produce 1 tonne (1000 kg) of aluminium? ....

ii) Australians used about 3 billion aluminium cans in 2002.
How many tonnes of aluminium does this represent?

....

iii) How many tonnes of bauxite were mined to supply Australians with aluminium cans in 2002?

....

b) Outline the environmental consequences of:

i) Mining the bauxite. ....

....

ii) Extracting the aluminium. ....

....

iii) Not recycling the cans. ....

....

Sustainable Development

Q1 Hydrogen is often talked about as the 'fuel of the future'.

a) What is produced when hydrogen is burnt?

....

b) Why is it better for the environment if hydrogen rather than petrol is burned?

....

c) Explain the problems that will have to be overcome before the public will be able to use hydrogen-powered vehicles on a large scale.

....

....

Think about storage of hydrogen and the costs involved.

....

Q2 Biogas is a mixture of methane (CH_4) and carbon dioxide. It is produced by microorganisms digesting waste material.

a) What products are formed when **biogas** is completely burnt?

....

b) What would be the main problem with using a **biogas generator** in a place like Siberia?

....

Q3 The diagram shows the production and use of one type of **biogas**.

a) Label the diagram by writing the correct letter next to each arrow:

   A CO_2 released into atmosphere

   B biogas generator

   C animal waste

   D CO_2 absorbed by grass during photosynthesis

   E methane $\rightarrow CO_2$

b) Explain why biogas is a renewable fuel.

....

c) Burning biogas releases CO_2 into the atmosphere. Explain how **producing** biogas **removes** CO_2 from the atmosphere.

....

....

Sustainable Development

Q4   In Brazil, **ethanol** produced by **fermenting sugar cane** is a popular fuel for vehicles. The ethanol is mixed with **petrol** before it is used to give a fuel known as **gasohol**.

a)   What is produced when **ethanol** (C_2H_5OH) is burnt?

....

b)   Using gasohol does not increase the amount of carbon dioxide in the atmosphere as much as using pure petrol does. Explain why not.

....

....

c)   Why would it be more difficult to produce large quantities of gasohol in the UK than it is in Brazil?

....

....

Q5   Alternative fuels such as **biogas** and **gasohol** have advantages and disadvantages compared with traditional fossil fuels.

Imagine you are writing a leaflet for a 'green' organisation promoting the use of alternative fuels like biogas and ethanol as a way of achieving sustainable development.

a)   Give four advantages of these fuels that you could use in favour of your argument.

1. ....

2. ....

3. ....

4. ....

b)   Suggest two points that someone who disagrees with you might put forward.

1. ....

....

2. ....

....

Top Tips: **Sustainable development** isn't all about loving trees and hugging bunnies, but about being sensible now so that our descendants don't have to live on raw rat meat and live underground to hide from all the **pollution** we've left behind. So think about them when you leave your TV on standby.

Novel Properties

Q1   **KEVLAR®** is a material that was originally invented to strengthen car tyres.
It is an extremely useful material which is now used for many **different purposes**.

Complete the table to show one **property** of KEVLAR® that makes it suitable for each given use.

USE	PROPERTY
Glass-worker's gloves	
Firefighter's helmets	
Canoes	
Bulletproof vests	

Q2   Many useful devices and materials were developed from **accidental discoveries**. One example is the glue used on **Post-it® Notes**, which was invented when scientists were trying to create a new glue to use on sticky tape.

    a)   Why was the new glue unsuitable for its original purpose?

    ....

    b)   What property of the new glue made it ideal for its eventual use on Post-it® Notes?

    ....

Q3   **Thinsulate™** is a new material that is an excellent **thermal insulator**.

    a)   How does the structure of Thinsulate™ make it a good thermal insulator?

    ....

    ....

    b)   Give one practical use of Thinsulate™. ....

Q4   GORE-TEX® is a brand of fabric. The pores in the **PTFE membrane** in **GORE-TEX®** fabric are much larger than **water molecules**, but much smaller than **water droplets**.

    a)   Explain the importance of this pore size in the function of clothing made from GORE-TEX® products.

    ....

    ....

    b)   As well as the PTFE membrane, GORE-TEX® products include a layer of another fabric, such as nylon. Explain why this is necessary.

    ....

Smart Materials

Q1   **Nitinol** is a shape memory alloy which has some properties that are unusual for metals.

a)   Explain why nitinol is a 'smart material'.

....

....

....

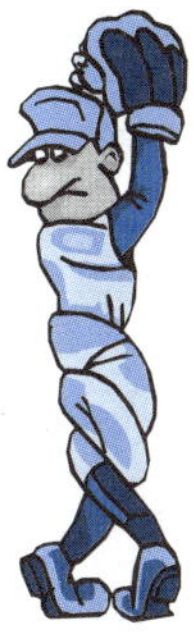

b)   What could nitinol be used for?

....

Q2   The packaging around some **fresh meat** has a coloured dot on it that gradually gets **darker**. The **speed** at which this happens depends on the **temperature**, as shown in this graph.

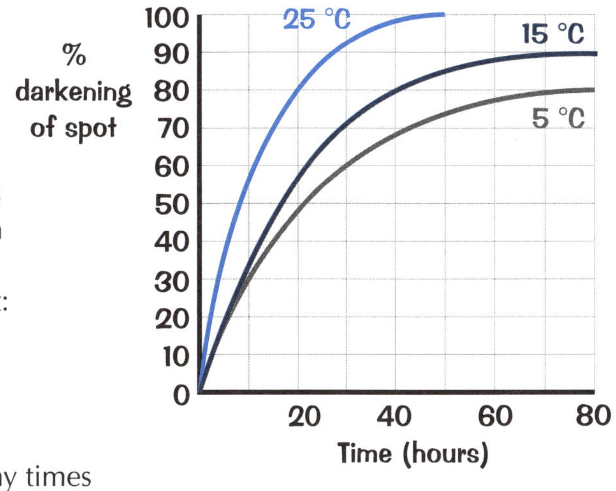

a)   When the dot is more than **80% dark**, the food is no longer safe to eat. The graph shows that when kept at **5 °C**, the food is safe to eat for up to **80 hours**. For how long is it safe to eat when kept at:

i)   15 °C? ....

ii)   25 °C? ....

b)   Use your answers to part a) to work out how many times faster the food goes off for every **10 °C** rise in temperature.

....

c)   Assuming this trend continues, how long would the food stay safe to eat if it was kept at **35 °C**?

....

d)   Explain how the darkening of the dot works.

....

....

Q3   Explain why chemicals called '**oxygen scavengers**' are sometimes added to packaged foods.

....

....

Smart Materials

Q4   **Silica gel** is a chemical that absorbs water. **Fresh orange peel** gradually releases water. In an experiment, three slices of **bread** (each with exactly the same mass) were sealed in airtight jars. One jar contained just the bread, one also contained some silica gel and the third contained some fresh orange peel. After a few days the amount of **mould** on each of the slices of bread was estimated. The results are shown below.

Contents of jar	% Surface of bread with mould
Bread and silica gel	5
Bread only	25
Bread and orange peel	65

a)   Name a controlled variable in this experiment.

....

b)   What is being changed by adding silica gel or orange peel?

....

c)   Why do the jars have to be sealed?

....

d)   What do the results tell you about the speed at which mould grows?

....

Q5   **Smart materials** can change their properties depending on the external conditions. Give **one possible use** of each of the smart materials described below.

a)   A dye that changes from red to green when it is cooled below a certain temperature.

....

b)   A material that expands when an electric current is passed through it and produces electricity when squeezed.

....

c)   A liquid that turns into a solid when exposed to a magnetic field.

....

d)   A dye that becomes more transparent as the light intensity decreases.

....

Nanotechnology

Q1 Complete the table below to show how **nanoparticles** can have different **properties** to the bulk chemical they're made from.

CHEMICAL	NANOPARTICLE PROPERTY	'BULK' CHEMICAL PROPERTY
Zinc oxide	Absorbs visible light	
Titanium dioxide	Absorbs visible light	
Silver		Doesn't affect microbes
Gold		Gold-coloured

Q2 **Nanoparticles** have the potential to be extremely **useful** materials. Describe one use of:

a) zinc oxide nanoparticles ....

b) silver nanoparticles ....

c) gold nanoparticles ....

Q3 **Titanium dioxide** is used as a pigment in white paint because it reflects visible light very strongly.

a) i) What size would you expect the titanium dioxide particles in the paint to be?

   A 1-100 nm   **B** 0.1-5 µm   **C** 10-100 mm

   ii) Give a reason for your choice.

   ....

   ....

b) Nanoparticles of titanium dioxide are used in sunscreens.
Match the properties of titanium dioxide nanoparticles to their benefit in sunscreen.

absorb visible light

reflect UV light

insoluble in water

stable under UV light

leaves no marks on the skin

not dissolved by sweat

prevents harmful rays reaching the skin

properties not changed by sunlight

Nanotechnology

Q4 Materials known as **nanocomposites** are now being developed.

a) What is a nanocomposite?

....

b) A concrete nanocomposite has been developed for use in building.

   i) Which nanomaterial does this nanocomposite contain?

....

   ii) What benefits are there in using the nanocomposite?

....

c) Give another example of how nanocomposites can be used to improve the properties of a material.

....

A nanocampsite

Q5 In an episode of the TV series 'Star Trek — The Next Generation', two **nanites** (robots smaller than living cells) escape from a genetics experiment and enter the computer system. They begin to **replicate** rapidly, **destroying** all the starship's essential systems.

a) How do real nanomachines differ from the fictional nanites described in the TV series?

....

b) Explain the advantages of developing nanomachines.

....

c) Scare stories in newspapers have negatively affected the public perception of nanotechnology. Describe some of the concerns raised by:

   i) the press and the general public.

....

....

   ii) scientists involved in the development of the new technology.

....

....

Top Tips: The discovery of all these bizarre properties of nanoparticles opened up huge new areas to investigate. Putting familiar materials to novel uses means technology that was once science-fiction is now a real possibility — all thanks to a bunch of tiny little particles. Hooray for nanoparticles.

Beer and Wine

Q1 Use the words in the box to fill in the gaps in the passage below about **fermentation**.
Each word may be used once, more than once, or not at all.

70 °C	hot	concentration	cold	enzymes	temperature	sugars 50 °C

Fermentation is used to turn .... into ethanol. The reaction happens

due to .... found in yeast. The .... needs to be

carefully controlled during the reaction — if it is too .... the reaction

is very slow, and if it is too .... the .... are

destroyed. The optimum is about ....

Q2 Mark met his friend John as he was leaving the pub. John had been **drinking** for several hours, and Mark noticed that he was **swaying** and that he **stumbled** several times as he walked away.

a) Explain why alcohol has this effect on the body.

....

b) Explain why it would be dangerous for John to drive home after his evening at the pub.

....

c) Alcohol can be dangerous in other ways, because excessive consumption leads to impaired judgement and lack of self-control. Suggest one way that this altered behaviour could be potentially harmful.

....

Q3 Answer the following questions about **fermentation**.

a) Which of the following is the correct equation for the production of ethanol? Circle A, B or C.

A $C_6H_{12}O_6 \rightarrow 2C_2H_5OH + 2CO_2$

B $C_6H_{12}O_6 \rightarrow 2C_2H_5OH + 2O_2$

C $C_6H_{12}O_6 \rightarrow 2C_2H_5OH + H_2O$

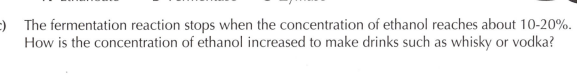

b) What is the name of the enzyme in yeast? Circle the correct letter.

A Ethanoate   B Fermentase   C Zymase

c) The fermentation reaction stops when the concentration of ethanol reaches about 10-20%. How is the concentration of ethanol increased to make drinks such as whisky or vodka?

....

Beer and Wine

Q4 Ethanol is produced using **fermentation**.

a) When producing ethanol, why is it important to stop oxygen getting into the fermentation mixture?

....

b) "The fermentation reaction stops when all the enzymes in the yeast are used up."
Is this statement true? Explain your answer.

....

....

Q5 Excessive **alcohol** intake can have **damaging effects** on the human body.

a) Alcohol can cause **dehydration**. What effect does this have on the brain?

....

b) Which other organ is often damaged by excessive alcohol intake?

....

c) Suggest an economic cost to society of excessive drinking.

....

Q6 Alcohol can be **addictive**, and an addiction to alcohol is known as **alcoholism**.
Explain the effect that being an alcoholic could have on:

a) A person's health.

....

....

b) Their personal and working life.

....

....

c) Society in general.

....

....

Top Tips: There's some evidence that a glass of red wine with your dinner may be good for you. In the newspaper headlines, that might appear as "Drinking's good for you", but never forget — drinking to excess can be a **disaster** — for your health, your family, your career, the world...

Emulsifiers and Properties

Q1 Jeremy is using some **oil-based paints**. One of the paints is too thick so he squeezes some into a small jar, adds a few drops of **water**, stirs it with his brush and then leaves it for five minutes.

a) Describe what Jeremy will see happening in the jar.

....

b) Explain why this happens.

....

c) What sort of substance could Jeremy add to the jar now to make the paint usable?

....

Q2 Complete the diagram to show an **emulsifier** in action.

a) Label the following on your diagram:

hydrophobic part   **oil**

emulsifier

hydrophilic part   **water**

b) Use the diagram to help you explain how emulsifiers help oil and water to mix.

....

....

Q3 Indicate whether the following statements are **true** or **false**.

		True	False
a)	An emulsion is made up of droplets of solid suspended in a liquid.	☐	☐
b)	The hydrophilic part of a molecule of emulsifier is attracted to water.	☐	☐
c)	The 'tail' of a molecule of emulsifier is the hydrophobic part.	☐	☐
d)	There is a natural emulsifier called lecithin in egg whites.	☐	☐

Q4 Look at the list of **materials** below and complete the table by selecting the best one to use for each of the **products** given. Give one **property** of each material that makes it suitable for use in the product you have chosen.

stainless steel   cotton   oak   glass

PRODUCT	MATERIAL	PROPERTY
Frying pan		
Window		
Cushion cover		
Bookcase		

Mixed Questions — C1b Topics 7 & 8

Q1   **Crude oil** is a mixture of **hydrocarbons**. They can be separated in the laboratory using small-scale **fractional distillation**, giving the fractions shown in the table.

fraction	boiling range (°C)	viscosity	flammability
petrol	20-70	runny	very flammable, clean yellow flame
naphtha	70-120	fairly runny	quite flammable, some smoke
kerosene	120-170	fairly viscous	harder to light, quite smoky flame
diesel	170-240	viscous	hard to light, very smoky flame

a)   Which fraction would you expect to contain hydrocarbon molecules with the **longest** carbon chains? Explain your answer.

....

b)   Hydrocarbons are often used as fuels.

i)   What is required for complete combustion of a hydrocarbon? ....

ii)   What two products would you expect from this reaction?

....

iii)   What two additional products would you expect from incomplete combustion?

....

c)   Describe three environmental problems that can be caused by burning hydrocarbons.

1. ....

2. ....

3. ....

d)   Another problem with fossil fuels like petrol is that they will run out one day. However other more sustainable fuels are available, e.g. alcohol.

i)   Describe how alcohol can be made from materials like sugar cane or barley.

....

....

ii)   Give the equation for the fermentation of the sugar glucose, $C_6H_{12}O_6$.

....

e)   Explain why recycling is an important part of sustainable development.

....

....

....

Mixed Questions — C1b Topics 7 & 8

Q2 Explain, using an example, how **intelligent packaging** can be used to:

a) slow down the growth of microorganisms. ....

....

b) monitor food and show when it's no longer safe to eat. ....

....

Q3 **Carbon fibre** and **LYCRA**® are both new materials with novel properties. Give one **use** of each material, and one **property** of the material that makes it suitable for that use.

Material	Use	Property
Carbon fibre		
LYCRA®		

Q4 Glyn is making home-made **mayonnaise**. The main ingredients are water, olive oil and **egg yolks**.

a) The egg yolks are used because they contain a substance called lecithin. What is lecithin?

....

b) Why is a substance like lecithin needed in the mayonnaise recipe?

....

....

c) The mayonnaise Glyn normally buys from the supermarket contains salt.

i) Explain how saltwater (brine) is split into different chemicals for use in the chemical industry.

....

....

ii) One of the products is sodium hydroxide. Give a use of sodium hydroxide.

....

Q5 The Earth's **atmosphere** has evolved over **millions of years**.

a) Explain how the early atmosphere, before green plants evolved, was different from today's.

....

b) Explain how past variations in the Earth's atmosphere could be used to argue that human activity may **not** be the cause of climate change.

....

....

Crude Oil

Q1 Which of these substances is **not** made from **crude oil**? Underline your answer.

plastics   solvents   metals   medicines   detergents

Q2 As crude oil is a **non-renewable** resource, people are keen to find **alternative** energy sources. Suggest a problem with each of these ways of using alternative fuels.

a) **Solar** energy for cars: ....

....

b) **Wind** energy to power an oven: ....

....

c) **Nuclear** energy for buses: ....

....

Q3 Forty years ago some scientists predicted that there would be no oil left by the year 2000, but obviously they were **wrong**. One reason is that modern engines are more **efficient** than in the past, so they use less fuel. Give two other reasons why the scientists' prediction was wrong.

1. ....

2. ....

Q4 Carbon is essential for life.

a) How many covalent bonds can a carbon atom form?

....

b) Explain how carbon allows complicated life forms like animals to exist.

....

....

....

Q5 Write a short paragraph summarising why crude oil is the most **common source** of fuel even though **alternatives** are available.

....

....

....

Alkanes and Alkenes

Q1 Complete this table showing the **molecular** and **displayed** formulae of some alkenes.

Alkene	Formula	Displayed formula
Ethene	a)	b)
c)	C_3H_6	d)

Q2 The general formula for **alkanes** is C_nH_{2n+2}. Use this to write down the formulae of these alkanes.

a) pentane (5 carbons) ....   b) hexane (6 carbons) ....

c) octane (8 carbons) ....   d) dodecane (12 carbons) ....

Q3 Tick the boxes to show whether the following statements are **true** or **false**.

                                                  True   False

a) Alkenes have double bonds between the hydrogen atoms. ☐ ☐

b) Alkenes are unsaturated. ☐ ☐

c) Alkenes can't form polymers as they have no spare bonds. ☐ ☐

d) Ethene has two carbon atoms. ☐ ☐

No, there's no spare 007s here.

Q4 Both **hexane** and **hexene** are colourless liquids.
Describe a test you could use to tell them apart.

....

....

Q5 The diagram shows a molecule that can be made from **ethene**.

$$\begin{array}{c} \quad \overset{\displaystyle H}{|} \quad \overset{\displaystyle H}{|} \\ H - C - C - OH \\ \quad \underset{\displaystyle H}{|} \quad \underset{\displaystyle H}{|} \end{array}$$

a) Name this molecule. ....

b) Which group of compounds does it belong to? ....

c) Describe how it is made industrially from ethene.

....

....

d) What name is given to this type of process? ....

Cracking Hydrocarbons

Q1   Fill in the gaps by choosing from the words in the box.

high	shorter	long	saturated	catalyst	cracking	diesel
		molecules	petrol	double bond		

There is more need for .... chain fractions of crude oil such as

.... than for longer chains such as ....·

Heating .... hydrocarbon molecules to ....

temperatures with a .... breaks them down

into smaller ....· This is called ....·

Q2   Circle the correct answer for each of the following questions.

a)   What type of chemical reaction is cracking?

A — Neutralisation   **B** — Displacement

C — Thermal decomposition   **D** — Redox

b)   Why are high temperatures needed to crack alkanes?

A — Catalysts only work when hot.   **B** — Energy is needed to break strong covalent bonds.

C — Large alkane molecules have strong forces between the molecules.

D — Alkenes are very unreactive hydrocarbons.

Q3   This apparatus can be used to crack a
liquid hydrocarbon such as **paraffin**.

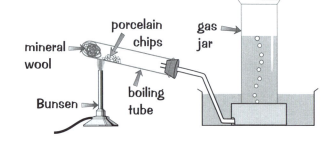

a)   Where would the paraffin be?

....

....

b)   What are the porcelain chips for? ....

c)   What collects at the cooler end of the boiling tube? ....

d)   What collects in the gas jar? ....

Cracking Hydrocarbons

Q4　Change this diagram into a **word equation** and a **symbol equation**.

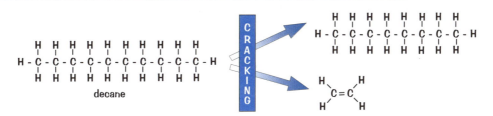

a)　Word equation:　..........................　→　..........................　+　..........................

b)　Symbol equation:　..........................　→　..........................　+　..........................

Q5　Diesel is **cracked** to produce products that are more in demand.

a)　A molecule produced when cracking diesel has the formula C_2H_4.

　　i)　What is the name of this hydrocarbon?　..

　　ii)　What is the main use of C_2H_4?　...

b)　Name another useful substance that can be produced when diesel is cracked.

　　..

Q6　Horatio owns a **crude oil refinery**. He records the amount of each fraction that's **present** in a sample of crude oil and compares it against how much of each fraction his customers want.

a)　Which fractions in this sample of crude oil are in excess (more is produced than can be sold)?

　　...

　　...

b)　For which fraction in this sample does the demand outweigh the supply by the greatest amount?

　　...

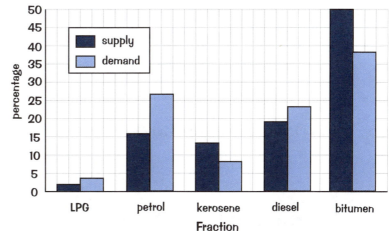

c)　Explain how cracking will help Horatio match the levels of supply to the levels of demand.

　　..

　　..

Top Tips:　Cracking is really useful, and dead important too. It helps us get the most out of crude oil, so we don't end up with loads of a fraction that we don't want or need. Hooray for cracking!

Vegetable Oils

Q1   Each diagram shows part of a fat structure. Draw lines to match each label to its correct structure.

Saturated animal fat

Polyunsaturated grape seed oil

Monounsaturated olive oil

Q2   **Cholesterol** is a substance made in the liver. **Oils** are often classed as healthy or not according to their effect on the amount of cholesterol in the blood.

   a)   Give a type of illness which is associated with high levels of cholesterol in the blood.

   ....

   b)   Put these types of oil in order of 'healthiness', with the most healthy first.

        saturated   polyunsaturated   monounsaturated

   ....

   c)   Explain what is meant by the terms **saturated** and **unsaturated**.

   ....

   d)   What is the difference between polyunsaturated and monounsaturated molecules?

   ....

   ....

   e)   What process is used to convert polyunsaturated oils into saturated fats?

   ....

Q3   **Margarine** is usually made from **partially hydrogenated** vegetable oil.

   a)   Describe the process of hydrogenation.

   ....

   ....

   b)   How does hydrogenation affect the melting points of vegetable oils?

   ....

Vegetable Oils

Q4 Complete the passage below using words from the list.

single   strong   inflexible   viscous   flexible   double   can   weak   straight   can't

Saturated oils contain long chains of carbon atoms joined by .... bonds. This makes them .... and ...., so they .... pack tightly together. The forces between these molecules are .... and so the oils are more ....

Q5 Circle the correct word from each pair.

Unsaturated oils have **double** / **triple** bonds between some of the carbon atoms. These make the molecule **kinked** / **straight** and **flexible** / **inflexible** and so they **can** / **can't** pack tightly together. The forces between these molecules are **strong** / **weak** and so the oils are **less** / **more** viscous.

Q6 Many people eat **margarine** and **low-fat spreads** (which are basically margarine and water) as a healthier alternative to butter. Below is part of the **nutritional information** on a packet of butter, a tub of margarine and a tub of low-fat spread. All values are per 100 g.

	BUTTER	MARGARINE	LOW-FAT SPREAD
ENERGY (kJ)	3031	2198	1396
SATURATED FAT (g)	54	19.5	8.7
MONOUNSATURATED FAT (g)	19.8	25.4	17.6
POLYUNSATURATED FAT (g)	2.6	11.4	7.0

saturated fat

a) Calculate the total amount of fat per 100 g of each product.

....

....

b) Calculate the percentage of the total fat in each product that is saturated.

....

....

c) What is the connection between the total amount of fat and the energy supplied by these products?

....

Top Tips: You need to make sure you know the differences between **saturated** and **unsaturated** oils. Then there's the **mono** and **poly**unsaturates. But it's less tricky than it sounds — learn about their properties and their effects on your health, and you'll soon be **saturated** with knowledge. Boom boom.

Plastics

Q1 Tick the box next to the **true** statement below.

☐ The monomer of poly(ethene) is ethene.

☐ The polymer of poly(ethene) is ethane.

☐ The monomer of poly(ethene) is ethane.

We bring you Gold, Frankincense...
and poly-myrrh

Q2 **Addition polymers** are formed when **unsaturated monomers** link together. Special conditions are needed to make this happen.

a) What feature of the monomer molecules makes them 'unsaturated'?

....

b) Name two of the 'special conditions' that are used in this reaction.

1. ....

2. ....

Q3 The diagram below shows the polymerisation of ethene to form **poly(ethene)**.

$$n \begin{pmatrix} H & H \\ | & | \\ C = C \\ | & | \\ H & H \end{pmatrix} \longrightarrow \begin{pmatrix} H & H \\ | & | \\ C - C \\ | & | \\ H & H \end{pmatrix}_n$$

many ethene molecules   poly(ethene)

a) Draw a similar diagram in the box below to show the polymerisation of **propene** (C_3H_6).

It's easier if you think of propene as
$$\begin{matrix} H & H \\ | & | \\ C = C \\ | & | \\ H & CH_3 \end{matrix}$$

b) Name the polymer you have drawn. ....

Plastics

Q4   Which of the following items is made from **expanded polystyrene**? Circle the correct answer.

packing material

carpets

ropes

crates

Q5   The diagram shows part of the chain of a **polyvinyl chloride** (**PVC**) molecule.

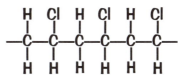

a)   Which of these formulae represents the monomer used to make PVC? Tick one box.

b)   Write a displayed equation in the box below to show the formation of PVC.

c)   The diagram below shows part of the chain of a polyphenylethene (polystyrene) molecule. Draw the monomer used to make this polymer in the space provided.

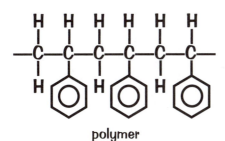
polymer

monomer

Properties of Plastics

A   **B**

Q1 **Polymer** molecules are **long chains**, as shown in the diagrams.

Which diagram shows a **thermosetting** polymer? Explain your answer.

....

....

Q2 When old houses are modernised, the **wooden window frames** are often replaced with new ones made from **PVC**.

a) Describe the physical properties of pure PVC.

....

b) Explain why preservatives are added to the PVC used to make window frames.

....

....

Q3 Two rulers, made from **different plastics**, were investigated by bending and heating them. The results are shown in the table.

	RESULT ON BENDING	RESULT ON HEATING
Ruler 1	Ruler bends easily and springs back into shape	Ruler becomes soft and then melts
Ruler 2	Ruler snaps in two	Ruler doesn't soften and eventually turns black

a) Which ruler is made from a polymer that has **strong** forces between its molecules? ....

b) The atoms in both types of plastic are held together with the same strong covalent bonds. Explain why one type of plastic melts and bends more easily than the other.

....

....

Q4 **Low density poly(ethene)** and **high density poly(ethene)** are both made from the same monomers, but have very different properties.

a) Explain what causes the different properties.

....

....

b) Poly(styrene) and poly(propene) have different properties. Why is this likely to be?

....

....

Uses of Plastics

Q1   From the list below circle any **properties** you think it is important for a plastic to have if it is to be used to make **Wellington boots**.

 low melting point

 lightweight

 waterproof

 rigid

 heat resistant

Q2   Complete the table to show the most suitable **use** of each polymer using the options in the list.

carrier bags   kettles   window frames   disposable cups

POLYMER	PROPERTIES	USE
polypropene	heat-resistant	
polystyrene foam	thermal insulator	
low density polyethene	lightweight	
PVC	strong, durable, rigid	

Each use can only be used once.

Q3   Two types of **polythene** are manufactured from ethene using different reaction conditions. One is **high density polythene** (**HDP**) and the other is **low density polythene** (**LDP**).

The table compares some of their properties.

	DENSITY	SOFTENING TEMP.	FLEXIBILITY
LDP	Low	Below 100 °C	High
HDP	High	Above 100 °C	Fairly low

For each of the following applications choose which type of polythene should be used and give a reason for your choice.

a)   toothpaste tubes ....

....

b)   freezer bags ....

....

c)   drain pipes ....

....

d)   hospital equipment that has to be sterilised ....

....

Uses of Plastics

Q4   Most plastics are not readily **biodegradable**.

a)   Lots of plastic is buried in landfill sites. Suggest one problem with this method of disposal.

....

b)   Another disposal method is to burn the waste plastic.
Why might there be a problem with the gases produced?

....

c)   Recycling plastics avoids the problems of disposal. What is the main problem with this solution?

....

Q5   Some carrier bags are made from **recycled polythene**.

a)   What is the raw material used to make plastics?

....

b)   Use what you know **about this raw material** to explain why it is a good idea to recycle plastics.

....

....

c)   Describe three types of degradable plastic which have been developed recently.

....

....

....

....

d)   Newly developed plastics have to be tested to see exactly
what is produced when they break down. Explain why.

....

e)   Things are often made from plastics because they are cheap. Why might this change in the future?

....

....

Top Tips: Plastics are really useful materials, and completely **man-made**. Well done us.
But there aren't any organisms that can **break them down**, and they're also made out of **crude oil**,
which is a bit of a shame. Maybe not quite so well done us.

Drug Synthesis

Q1   Read the passage below and answer the questions that follow.

In 1763 a scientific paper was written describing the success of an extract of willow bark in treating fevers (high temperatures). It was later discovered that the bark contained a substance called salicylic acid, and for a hundred years this was used to treat fevers and rheumatism. Unfortunately, it was unpleasant to take and caused stomach and mouth ulcers. Because of this, many people couldn't take it.

In 1899 a substance called aspirin was first marketed. A known reaction — esterification — was used to modify the structure of salicylic acid. Aspirin had the useful properties of salicylic acid but fewer of the unpleasant side effects.

a)   What unwanted side effects did salicylic acid have?

....

b)   Give one way that aspirin can be produced.

....

c)   Why do you think that this method of producing aspirin was tried?

....

d)   What were the benefits of the new drug, aspirin?

....

Q2   It's not just guess-work when chemists are creating new chemicals.

a)   Why do chemists use information about known reactions when making new drugs?

....

....

b)   Why is this method of drug synthesis better than if chemists guessed when creating chemicals.

....

....

c)   What are the difficulties faced when creating and marketing new drugs?

....

....

Drug Synthesis

Q3 Before use, drugs go through a long process of **testing**.
Put the steps below in order to show the correct sequence of such tests.

A Large groups of patients are tested, with some of them being given a placebo.

B The drug is tested on cultures of living cells and on animals.

C Healthy human volunteers are given the drug in slowly increasing amounts.

D Small groups of people with the disease are tested.

Order: ....

Q4 Most modern drugs are made by a process called **staged synthesis**.

a) Describe how a drug **ABC** could be made by staged synthesis from compounds A, B and C.

....

....

b) How would a drug company make a 'family' of new drugs similar to ABC?

....

....

Q5 A drug company wants to make a **family** of compounds similar to a successful new drug, **PQR**.
They have 2 **P-type** compounds (P1 and P2), 2 **Q-type** compounds (Q1 and Q2) and 2 **R-type** compounds (R1 and R2).

a) List the possible combinations to show how they could make eight new compounds.

....

....

b) Calculate how many compounds the company could make if they had 15 of each type.

....

....

Relative Formula Mass

Q1 a) What is meant by the **relative atomic mass** of an element?

....

b) What are the **relative atomic masses (A_r)** of the following:

i) magnesium .... **iv)** hydrogen .... **vii)** K ....

ii) neon .... **v)** C .... **viii)** Ca ....

iii) oxygen .... **vi)** Cu .... **ix)** Cl ....

Q2 **Identify** the **elements** A, B and C.

Element A is ....

Element B is ....

Element C is ....

> Element A has an A_r of 4.
> Element B has an A_r 3 times that of element A.
> Element C has an A_r 4 times that of element A.

Q3 a) Explain how the **relative formula mass** of a **compound** is calculated.

....

b) What are the **relative formula masses (M_r)** of the following:

i) water (H_2O) ....

ii) potassium hydroxide (KOH) ....

iii) nitric acid (HNO_3) ....

iv) sulphuric acid (H_2SO_4) ....

v) ammonium nitrate (NH_4NO_3) ....

vi) aluminium sulphate ($Al_2(SO_4)_3$) ....

Q4 The equation below shows a reaction between an element, X, and water. The total M_r of the products is **114**. What is substance X?

$$2X + 2H_2O \rightarrow 2XOH + H_2$$

....

....

C2 Topic 5 — Synthesis

Empirical Formulae

Q1 What is the **empirical formula** of each of these substances?

a) H_2O_2 ....

b) H_2O ....

c) C_2H_4 ....

d) C_4H_8 ....

e) CH_3COOH ....

Q2 A hydrocarbon contains 6 g of **carbon** and 2 g of **hydrogen**. Calculate its **empirical formula**.

....

....

....

Q3 1.48 g of a **calcium compound** contains 0.8 g calcium, 0.64 g oxygen and 0.04 g hydrogen.

Work out the empirical formula of the compound.

....

....

....

Q4 16 g of **copper** makes 20 g of **copper oxide**. Calculate the **empirical formula** of copper oxide.

....

....

....

Q5 A sugar found in honey contains **40% carbon**, **6.67% hydrogen** and **53.33% oxygen**.

a) Calculate its empirical formula.

....

....

....

b) The molecular mass of the sugar is 180. What is its molecular formula?

....

....

Calculating Masses in Reactions

Q1 Anna burns **10 g** of **magnesium** in air to produce **magnesium oxide** (MgO).

a) Write out the **balanced equation** for this reaction.

....

b) Calculate the mass of **magnesium oxide** that's produced.

....

....

....

Q2 What mass of **sodium** is needed to make **2 g** of **sodium oxide**? $4Na + O_2 \rightarrow 2Na_2O$

....

....

....

Q3 **Aluminium** and **iron oxide** (Fe_2O_3) react together to produce **aluminium oxide** (Al_2O_3) and **iron**.

a) Write out the **balanced equation** for this reaction.

....

b) What **mass** of iron is produced from **20 g** of iron oxide?

....

....

....

Q4 When heated, **limestone** ($CaCO_3$) decomposes to form **calcium oxide** (CaO) and **carbon dioxide**.

How many **kilograms** of limestone are needed to make **100 kilograms** of **calcium oxide**?

The calculation is the same — just use 'kg' instead of 'g'.

....

....

....

....

Calculating Masses in Reactions

Q5 **Iron oxide** is reduced to **iron** inside a blast furnace using carbon. There are **three** stages involved.

Stage A	$C + O_2 \rightarrow CO_2$
Stage B	$CO_2 + C \rightarrow 2CO$
Stage C	$3CO + Fe_2O_3 \rightarrow 2Fe + 3CO_2$

a) If **10 g** of **carbon** are used in stage B, and all the carbon monoxide produced gets used in stage C, what **mass** of CO_2 is produced in **stage C**?

....

....

....

....

Work out the mass of CO at the end of stage B first.

b) Suggest what happens to the CO_2 produced in stage C.

....

Look at where CO_2 is used.

Q6 **Sodium sulphate** (Na_2SO_4) is made by reacting **sodium hydroxide** (NaOH) with **sulphuric acid** (H_2SO_4). **Water** is also produced.

a) Write out the **balanced equation** for this reaction.

....

b) What mass of **sodium hydroxide** is needed to make **75 g** of **sodium sulphate**?

....

....

....

....

c) What mass of **water** is formed when **50 g** of **sulphuric acid** reacts with sodium sulphate?

....

....

....

....

> **_Top Tips:_** Masses, equations, formulae — they can all seem a bit scary. But don't worry, practice makes perfect. And once you get the hang of them you'll wonder what all the fuss was about.

Atom Economy

Q1 **Copper oxide** can be reduced to copper by heating it with carbon.

> **copper oxide + carbon → copper + carbon dioxide**
>
> **2CuO + C → 2Cu + CO$_2$**

a) What is the useful product in this reaction? ....

b) Calculate the atom economy.

$$\text{atom economy} = \frac{\text{total M}_r \text{ of useful products}}{\text{total M}_r \text{ of reactants}} \times 100$$

....

....

c) What percentage of the starting materials are wasted?

....

Q2 It is important in industry to find the **best atom economy**.

a) Explain why. ....

....

....

b) What types of reaction have the highest atom economies? Give an example.

....

Q3 **Titanium** can be reduced from titanium chloride (TiCl$_4$) using magnesium or sodium.

a) Work out the atom economy for the reaction:

i) with magnesium: TiCl$_4$ + 2Mg → Ti + 2MgCl$_2$ ....

....

ii) with sodium: TiCl$_4$ + 4Na → Ti + 4NaCl ....

....

b) Which one has the better atom economy? ....

Q4 **Chromium** can be extracted from its oxide (Cr$_2$O$_3$) using **aluminium**.
The products of the reaction are **aluminium oxide** and **chromium**.

Calculate the atom economy of this reaction.

....

....

72

Percentage Yield

Q1 James wanted to produce **silver chloride** (AgCl). He added a carefully measured mass of silver nitrate to an excess of dilute hydrochloric acid.

a) Write down the formula for calculating the **percentage yield** of a reaction?

....

b) James calculated that he should get 2.7 g of silver chloride, but he only got 1.2 g. What was the **percentage yield**?

....

Q2 Aaliya and Natasha mixed together barium chloride ($BaCl_2$) and sodium sulphate (Na_2SO_4) in a beaker. An **insoluble** substance formed. They **filtered** the solution to obtain the solid substance, and then transferred the solid to a clean piece of **filter paper** and left it to dry.

a) Aaliya calculated that they should produce a yield of **15 g** of barium sulphate. However, after completing the experiment they found they had only obtained **6 g**.

Calculate the **percentage yield** for this reaction.

....

b) Suggest two reasons why their actual yield was lower than their predicted yield.

1. ....

....

2. ....

....

Q3 The reaction between magnesium and oxygen produces a white powder, **magnesium oxide**. Four samples of magnesium, each weighing 2 g, were burned and the oxide produced was weighed. The **expected** yield was **3.33 g**.

Sample	Mass of oxide (g)
A	3.00
B	3.18
C	3.05
D	3.15

a) What is the percentage yield for each sample?

....

....

....

b) Which of the following are likely reasons why the yield was not 100%? Circle their letters.

A The reaction was too fast **B** Too much magnesium was burned

C The magnesium was not pure **D** Some of the oxide was lost before it was weighed

C2 Topic 5 — Synthesis

Percentage Yield

Q4   The reaction used to make **ammonia** by the **Haber process** is represented by the equation:

$$N_2 + 3H_2 \rightleftharpoons 2NH_3$$

a)   What does the $\rightleftharpoons$ symbol mean? ....

b)   Why will this reaction never give a 100% yield?

....

....

c)   To get the best yield a low temperature is needed.
Suggest why a very low temperature is **not** used in industry.

....

Q5   Complete the table of results showing the **percentage yields** from different experiments.

You can use the space below for working out.

Yield	Expected yield	Percentage yield
3.4 g	4.0 g	a)
6.4 g	7.2 g	b)
3.6 g	c)	80%
d)	6.5 g	90%

Q6   Limestone is mainly **calcium carbonate**. If calcium carbonate is heated it leaves solid **calcium oxide**. When **100 tonnes** of limestone were heated, **42 tonnes** of calcium oxide were produced.

a)   Write the equation for this reaction. ....

b)   What was the expected yield?   Use a periodic table to help you with this question.

....

....

c)   Using your answer from part b), calculate the percentage yield.

....

d)   Why are you unlikely ever to get a 100% yield from this process?

....

....

C2 Topic 5 — Synthesis

Isotopes and Relative Atomic Mass

Q1 Choose the correct words to complete this paragraph.

electrons	element	isotopes	protons	compound	neutrons

.... are different atomic forms of the same .... which have

the same number of .... but different numbers of ....

Q2 Which of the following atoms are **isotopes** of each other? Explain how you know.

W $^{12}_{6}C$ **X** $^{40}_{18}Ar$ **Y** $^{14}_{6}C$ **Z** $^{40}_{20}Ca$

.... and .... because ....

Q3 **Carbon-14** is an unstable isotope of carbon.

a) How many of the following particles does one atom of carbon-14 contain?

i) neutrons ....   **ii)** protons ....   **iii)** electrons ....

b) Carbon-12 is the more common isotope of carbon.
Would you expect it to have different chemical properties from carbon-14? Explain your answer.

....

Q4 Draw lines to join the beginning of each sentence to its correct ending.

Relative atomic mass is

Relative abundance means

the proportion of one isotope in an element

the average mass of all atoms of that element

Q5 **Chlorine** has two main **isotopes**, ^{35}Cl and ^{37}Cl. Their relative abundances are shown in the table.

relative mass of isotope	relative abundance
35	3
37	1

Use this information to calculate the relative atomic mass of chlorine.

....

....

More About the Periodic Table

Q1 Choose from the elements given below to answer the following questions.

iodine   nickel   silicon   sodium   radon   krypton   calcium

a) Which two are in the same group? .... and ....

b) Name an alkali metal. ....

c) Name a noble gas. ....

d) Name an element with seven electrons in its outer shell. ....

e) Name a non-metal which is not in group 0. ....

Q2 Circle the correct word from each pair to complete the sentences below.

a) The periodic table is made up of all the known **compounds** / **elements**.

b) The periodic table shows the elements in order of ascending atomic **mass** / **number**.

c) Elements in the same **group** / **period** have the same number of electrons in their outer shells.

d) Each **column** / **row** in the periodic table contains elements with similar properties.

e) There are **less** / **more** than 100 known elements.

Q3 Some elements undergo **similar reactions** to each other.

a) Tick the pairs of elements that would undergo similar reactions.

A potassium and rubidium ☐   **C** calcium and oxygen ☐

B helium and fluorine ☐   **D** calcium and magnesium ☐

Stop copying...

b) Explain why elements in the **same group** undergo similar reactions.

....

....

Q4 Complete this table.

	Alternative Name for Group	Number of Electrons in Outer Shell
Group I	Alkali metals	
Group VII		7
Group 0		*

* excluding helium

Electron Shells

Q1 a) Tick the boxes to show whether each statement is **true** or **false**.

True False

    i) Electrons orbit the nucleus in energy levels called shells. ☐ ☐

    ii) The highest energy levels are always filled first. ☐ ☐

    iii) The lowest energy levels are closest to the nucleus. ☐ ☐

    iv) Atoms are most stable when they have partially filled shells. ☐ ☐

    v) A maximum of eight electrons can occupy the first shell. ☐ ☐

b) Write out corrected versions of the **false** statements.

....

....

....

Q2 Identify **two** things that are wrong with this diagram.

1. ....

2. ....

Q3 Write out the **electronic configurations** of the following elements.

a) Beryllium ....   **d)** Calcium ....

b) Oxygen ....   **e)** Aluminium ....

c) Silicon ....   **f)** Argon ....

Q4 Are the following groups of elements **reactive** or **unreactive**? Explain why in each case.

a) Noble gases ....

....

b) Alkali metals ....

....

Q5 Describe the link between an element's position in the periodic table and the number of electrons it has in its outer shell.

....

....

Electron Shells

Q6 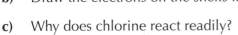 **Chlorine** has an atomic number of 17.

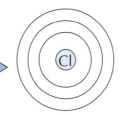

    a) What is its electron configuration? ....

    b) Draw the electrons on the shells in the diagram.

    c) Why does chlorine react readily?

....

Q7 Draw the **full electronic arrangements** for these elements. (The first three have been done for you.)

Hydrogen

Helium

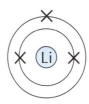

Lithium

a) Carbon

b) Nitrogen

c) Fluorine

d) Sodium

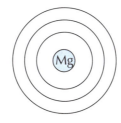

e) Magnesium

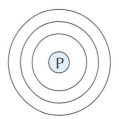

f) Phosphorus

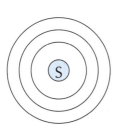

g) Sulphur

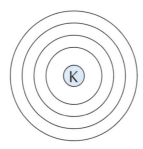

h) Potassium

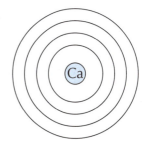

i) Calcium

Top Tips: Once you've learnt the '**electron shell rules**' these are pretty easy — the first shell can only take **two** electrons, and the second and third shells a maximum of **eight** each. Don't forget it.

Ionic Bonding

Q1   **True** or **false**?

		True	False

a)   In ionic bonding, ions lose or gain electrons to give atoms.   ☐ ☐

b)   Ions with opposite charges attract each other.   ☐ ☐

c)   Elements that lose electrons form positive ions.   ☐ ☐

d)   Elements that gain electrons form cations.   ☐ ☐

e)   Atoms form ions so that they can have full outer shells.   ☐ ☐

Q2   Use the **diagram** to answer the following questions.

a)   Which group of the periodic table does sodium belong to?   ....

b)   How many electrons does chlorine need to gain in order to have a full outer shell?   ....

c)   What is the charge on a sodium ion?   ....

d)   What is the chemical formula of sodium chloride?   ....

Q3   Here are some **elements** and the **ions** they form:

Make sure the charges on the ions balance.

beryllium, Be^{2+} potassium, K^+ iodine, I^- sulphur, S^{2-}

Write down the formulae of four compounds which can be made using just these elements.

1. ....

2. ....

3. ....

4. ....

Ionic Bonding

Q4 Elements react in order to get a **full outer shell** of electrons.

a) How many electrons does magnesium need to **lose** to get a full outer shell? ....

b) How many electrons does oxygen need to **gain** to get a full outer shell?   ....

c) Draw a 'dot and cross' diagram in the space provided to show what happens to the outer shells of electrons when magnesium and oxygen react.

The diagrams in question 2 are 'dot and cross' diagrams.

d) What is the chemical formula of magnesium oxide? ....

Q5 Atoms can **gain** or **lose** electrons to get a full outer shell.

a) How many electrons do the following elements need to **lose** in order to get a **full outer shell**?

i) Lithium ....

ii) Calcium ....

iii) Potassium ....

b) How many electrons do the following elements need to **gain** in order to get a **full outer shell**?

i) Oxygen ....

ii) Chlorine ....

iii) Fluorine ....

Q6 **Aluminium** is in **Group 3** of the periodic table.
Complete the following sentences by choosing the correct word from each pair.

a) An atom of aluminium has **three** / **five** electrons in its outer shell.

b) It will form an ion by **gaining** / **losing** these electrons.

c) The charge on an aluminium ion will be **3+** / **3−**.

d) The formula of the compound it makes with chloride ions (Cl^-) will be: $\mathbf{AlCl_3}$ / $\mathbf{Al_3Cl}$.

e) The formula of the compound it makes with oxide ions (O^{2-}) will be $\mathbf{Al_2O_3}$ / $\mathbf{Al_3O_2}$.

Ionic Compounds

Q1   Use a 'dot and cross' diagram to show how **sodium** and **oxygen** react to give **sodium oxide**.

Q2   Explain how sodium and chlorine atoms react to form the ionic compound **sodium chloride**.

....

....

Q3   Use 'dot and cross' diagrams to explain why **potassium chloride** has the formula **KCl** but **magnesium chloride** has the formula **MgCl₂**.

Ionic Compounds

Q4 **Sodium chloride** (table salt) is a hard, crystalline substance.

a) What name is given to the arrangement of the atoms in a crystal of sodium chloride?

....

b) Why can't sodium chloride conduct electricity when it is solid?

....

c) Circle the correct words to explain why sodium chloride has a high melting point.

> Sodium chloride has very **strong** / **weak** chemical bonds between the
> **negative** / **positive** sodium ions and the **negative** / **positive** chlorine ions.
> This means that it needs a **small** / **large** amount of energy to break the bonds.

Q5 Mike carries out an experiment to find out if **potassium chloride** conducts electricity. He tests the compound when it's solid, when it's dissolved in water and when it's molten.

a) Complete the following table of results.

	Conducts electricity?
When solid	
When dissolved in water	
When molten	

b) Explain your answers to part a).

....

....

....

Q6 The melting point of **calcium chloride** is **772 °C** and that of **carbon chloride** is **−23 °C**.

a) Which one is an ionic compound? Explain your choice.

....

b) Which one will conduct electricity when melted? Why does it conduct?

....

Reactivity Trends

Q1 Complete the paragraph below using words from the list.

outer   electrons   group   same   positively   negatively   inner   shielded   increases   decreases

Atoms in the same .... of the periodic table have the .... number of .... in their outer shells. As you go down a group the distance between the .... electrons and the .... charged nucleus .... The outer electrons are said to be .... by the .... shells.

Q2 Draw lines to match up the three parts of each of the sentences below.

Alkali metals	do not form ions	because they have 7 electrons in their outer shells
Halogens	lose electrons	because they have full outer shells
Noble gases	gain electrons	because they have 1 electron in their outer shells

Q3 Diagrams 1, 2 and 3 show the outer electrons of three atoms from the **same group**.

a) Which group are the atoms from? ....

b) What do all of the above atoms need to do to form ions?

....

c) **i)** Which atom from this group would you expect to form an ion most easily? ....

ii) Why does it form ions more easily than the others? ....

....

Q4 Atoms of **lithium**, **sodium** and **potassium** have **3**, **11** and **19 electrons** respectively.

a) Draw the electronic structure of each of these atoms in the space below.

b) State which of the three will be the most reactive and explain why.

....

....

Metals

Q1 The table shows the **properties** of some **elements**.

Element	Melting pt. (°C)	Boiling pt. (°C)	Electrical conductivity	Hardness
1	1903	2642	Good	Hard
2	114	444	None	Soft
3	1539	2887	Good	Hard
4	63	766	Good	Soft
5	3300	4827	Poor	Soft

Which of the elements 1 to 5 do you think are metals? ....

Q2 This table shows some of the **properties** of four different **metals**.

Metal	Heat conduction	Cost	Resistance to corrosion	Strength
1	average	high	excellent	good
2	average	medium	good	excellent
3	excellent	low	good	good
4	low	high	average	poor

Some metal is heavy.

Use the information in the table to choose which metal would be **best** for making:

a) Saucepan bases ....

b) Car bodies ....

c) A statue for a town centre ....

> Think about how long a statue would have to last for.

Q3 All metals have a similar **structure**. This explains why many of them have similar **properties**.

a) Draw a labelled diagram of a typical metal structure, showing the electrons.

b) What is unusual about the electrons in a metal?

....

Metals

Q4 24-carat gold is **pure** gold. 9-carat gold contains **9 parts** gold to 15 parts other metal. 9-carat gold is **harder** and **cheaper** than 24-carat gold.

a) What percentage of 9-carat gold is actually gold?

....

b) Why is 9-carat gold harder than pure gold? ....

....

....

Q5 **Alloys** are very useful materials.

Tonight Matthew, I'm going to be... steel.

a) Write a definition of the term **alloy**.

....

....

b) Complete the following sentences about alloys using the metals below.

iron   copper   silver   tin   titanium

i) Bronze is an alloy that contains copper and ....

ii) Cupronickel, which is used in 'silver' coins, contains nickel and ....

iii) Steel is an alloy made from carbon and ....

c) Give an example of how alloying a metal can change its properties.

....

....

Q6 **Gold** can be hammered into a sheet (called gold leaf) that's so **thin** you can see through it. Complete the following sentences by circling the correct word in each pair.

a) Gold leaf can be made because gold is very **malleable** / **tactile**.

b) Thin sheets of glass have to be made by pouring molten glass because glass is **malleable** / **brittle**.

c) Metals are malleable because the layers of **molecules** / **atoms** can slide over each other.

Top Tips: There are just two things that are really important here — the structure and properties of metals. Make sure you know how the structure of a metal is related to its properties, and also about how you can mix a metal with other things to change its properties. Easy peasy.

Electrolysis and the Half-Equations

Q1   Draw lines to join these words with their correct meanings.

Electrolysis

Electrolyte

Anode

Cathode

Cation

Anion

The positive electrode.

The breakdown of a substance using electricity.

Positive ion that is attracted to the cathode.

Negative ion that is attracted to the anode.

The negative electrode.

The liquid that is used in electrolysis.

Q2   Are these statements about the extraction of **aluminium** true or false?

		True	False
a)	Substances can only be electrolysed if molten or in solution.	☐	☐
b)	In the extraction of aluminium the electrolyte is molten aluminium metal.	☐	☐
c)	Aluminium is extracted from its ore, bauxite.	☐	☐
d)	Oxygen gas is given off during the extraction of aluminium by electrolysis.	☐	☐
e)	Aluminium is collected at the anode.	☐	☐

Q3   From the substances listed in the box below, write down those that:

> **copper,   copper sulphate crystals,   dilute sulphuric acid,   seawater,   alcohol,   table salt**

a)   can never be electrolysed ....

b)   can be electrolysed as they are ....

c)   can only be electrolysed when melted or dissolved in water

....

Q4   Complete this table to show the results of the **electrolysis** of some **molten substances**.

Salt	Anode product	Cathode product
Sodium chloride		
Calcium iodide		
Silver bromide		

Electrolysis and the Half-Equations

Q5 The diagram below shows the electrolysis of **molten aluminium oxide**.

Write the labels that should go at points A–G:

A ....

B ....

C ....

D ....

E ....

F ....

G ....

Q6 **Lead bromide** is an ionic substance. It doesn't easily dissolve in water.

a) How could lead bromide be made into a liquid for electrolysis?

....

b) Write **balanced** half-equations for the processes that occur at the cathode and anode during the electrolysis of lead bromide.

Lead ions have a 2+ charge. And remember, bromide ions pair up to become bromine molecules (Br_2).

Cathode: ....

Anode: ....

Q7 Write **half-equations** to show what happens at each electrode when these salts are electrolysed.

a) Potassium chloride, KCl

Cathode: .... Anode: ....

b) Calcium bromide, $CaBr_2$

Cathode: .... Anode: ....

c) Sodium fluoride, NaF

Cathode: .... Anode: ....

Top Tips: All I can say is, don't get the **cathode** and the **anode** mixed up. The cathode is the **negative** electrode and it attracts the **cations**, which are the positive ions. The anode is **positive** and so attracts **anions**, which are negative. It's easy to get confused, so make sure you know it properly now.

Mixed Questions — C2 Topics 5 & 6

Q1   Carbon contains the isotopes **carbon-12** and **carbon-14**.

a)   Write down the number of **protons**, **electrons** and **neutrons** in carbon-12.

.... protons .... neutrons .... electrons

b)   Most cars burn fuels containing carbon. The exhaust gases from the engine contain small amounts of carbon monoxide, CO.

i)   Calculate the relative formula mass of carbon monoxide.

....

ii)   Carbon monoxide reacts slowly with oxygen, O_2, to form carbon dioxide, CO_2.

$$2CO\ (g)\ +\ O_2\ (g)\ \rightarrow\ 2CO_2\ (g)$$

If 280 g of CO reacts with excess oxygen, what mass of **carbon dioxide** will be produced?

....

....

Q2   **Ethene** (C_2H_4) is an **unsaturated** molecule.

a)   i)   Draw the structure of a molecule of ethene, showing all the bonds.

ii)   Describe a test that would distinguish between ethane and ethene.
Give the result of the test for each substance.

....

....

b)   **Hydrogenated vegetable oils** are used in many foods. Explain what 'hydrogenation' means.

....

c)   Which of the following best explains why vegetable oils are hydrogenated? Circle one letter.

A It makes the oils better for your health.   B It gives the oils a firmer consistency.

C It gives the oils a more appealing taste.   D It makes the oils look more appetising.

Q3   Drug companies use **staged synthesis** to make a 'family' of very similar compounds.
These can then all be tested at once to see if any of them will make an **effective drug**.
Explain the advantage of doing this.

....

....

88

Mixed Questions — C2 Topics 5 & 6

Q4   The table shows the **uses** of some different **plastics** and the **monomers** used to make them.

monomer		polymer	use for polymer
ethene	H $C=C$ H H H	poly(ethene) $\left(\begin{array}{c} H\ H \\ C-C \\ H\ H \end{array}\right)_n$	
propene	H $C=C$ H H CH_3		rope
styrene	H $C=C$ H H O		

a)   Complete the table.

b)   Polythene is a flexible plastic. Explain what this tells you about the forces between its molecules.

....

c)   Would you expect polythene to have a low or a high melting point? Explain your answer.

....

Q5   8.1 g of a compound contains 4.9 g magnesium and 3.2 g oxygen. What is its **empirical formula**?

....

....

Q6   The first three elements in **Group I** of the **periodic table** are lithium, sodium and potassium.

a)   Write down the electron configurations for these three elements. (Use the periodic table to help you.)

....

b)   Describe and explain how the reactivity of these elements changes as you move down the group.

....

....

Q7   **Fermentation** is used to produce alcohol from sugars: $C_6H_{12}O_6 \rightarrow 2C_2H_5OH + 2CO_2$.
Calculate the **atom economy** of this reaction.

....

....

Mixed Questions — C2 Topics 5 & 6

Q8 Crude oil is a mixture of **saturated** and **unsaturated hydrocarbons**.

   a) Ethane (C_2H_6) is a saturated hydrocarbon.

      i) Draw the structure of a molecule of ethane, showing all the bonds.

     ii) What are saturated hydrocarbons known as? ....

   b) Short-chain hydrocarbons like ethane and ethene can be made from less useful long-chain hydrocarbons. Explain how this is done in industry (including the reaction conditions).

   ....

   ....

Q9 **Properties** of materials are related to the type of **bonding** in the molecules.

   a) Explain why **iron** is strong and conducts electricity.

   ....

   ....

   b) Explain how the properties of **sodium chloride** are related to the bonding within it.

   ....

   ....

Q10 An **electric current** is passed through **liquid lead bromide**, as shown in the diagram.

   a) What is this process called?

   ....

   b) Why does the lead bromide have to be liquid?

   ....

   ....

   c) Lead bromide, $PbBr_2$, is composed of Pb^{2+} and Br^- ions.

      i) State which ion moves toward each electrode during this process.

      Electrode A ....   Electrode B ....

     ii) Balance the following half equations for the reactions.

       $Pb^{2+} +$ $e^- \rightarrow$ Pb $Br^- \rightarrow$ $Br_2 +$ e^-

Covalent Bonding

Q1 Indicate whether each statement below is **true** or **false**.

		True	False
a)	Covalent bonding involves sharing electrons.	☐	☐
b)	Atoms with a full outer shell are more stable.	☐	☐
c)	Some atoms can make both ionic and covalent bonds.	☐	☐
d)	A hydrogen atom can form two covalent bonds.	☐	☐
e)	A carbon atom can form four covalent bonds.	☐	☐

Q2 **Complete** the following table to show how many extra electrons are needed to **fill up** the **outer shells** of these atoms.

Atom	Carbon	Chlorine	Hydrogen	Nitrogen
Number of electrons needed to fill outer shell				

Q3 Complete the following diagrams by adding **electrons** to the outer shells.

a) Hydrogen chloride (HCl)

b) Hydrogen (H_2)

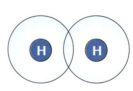

c) Carbon dioxide (CO_2)

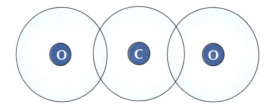

d) Water (H_2O)

Covalent Bonding

Q4 The **structural formula** of methane is shown in the diagram.

a) What **can't** the structural formula tell you about the structure of a molecule?

....

....

b) What type of diagram of a methane molecule would give you extra information?

....

c) Why might it be important to have this extra information?

....

Q5 **Oxygen** atoms make **covalent bonds** with atoms of various elements.

a) How many extra electrons does an atom gain by making a single covalent bond? ....

b) How many electrons are there in the outer shell of an oxygen atom? ....

c) How many more electrons does an oxygen atom need to gain in order to fill its outer shell?

....

d) How many covalent bonds must an oxygen atom make to have a full outer shell of electrons?

....

Q6 Atoms form bonds to gain a **full outer shell** of electrons.

a) Hydrogen atoms can only make one covalent bond.

How many hydrogen atoms will an oxygen atom bond with before it has a full outer shell of electrons?

don't go...

....

b) A molecule of carbon dioxide contains just one carbon atom and two oxygen atoms, yet carbon atoms need to gain a total of four electrons to fill their outer shells.

Explain how these atoms bond together so that they all have full outer shells of electrons.

....

....

Top Tips: You need to know why some elements bond covalently and what **properties** molecules have when they've bonded this way. Those dot and cross diagrams are pretty important too.

Molecular Substances: the Halogens

Q1 Fill in the blanks in the following paragraph by choosing words from the list.

weak   hard   small   easy   large   strong

> Simple molecular substances are made from .... molecules. The covalent bonds
>
> that hold the atoms together are .... but the forces between the molecules are quite
>
> .... Because of this it is fairly .... to separate the molecules.

Q2 Hydrogen and chlorine share electrons to form a molecule called **hydrogen chloride**.

Predict two properties that hydrogen chloride will have.

1. ....

2. ....

Q3 Complete the following sentences by circling the correct option, and explain your answers.

a) The melting and boiling points of simple molecular substances are **low** / **high**.

....

b) Simple molecular substances **conduct** / **don't conduct** electricity.

....

Q4 The table below shows the **atomic numbers** and **melting points** for three **halogens**.

Halogen	Atomic no.	Melting pt.
Fluorine	9	$-220\,°C$
Bromine	35	$-7\,°C$
Iodine	53	$114\,°C$

a) Plot the data on the axes given.

b) Describe the relationship between atomic number and melting point for the halogens.

....

....

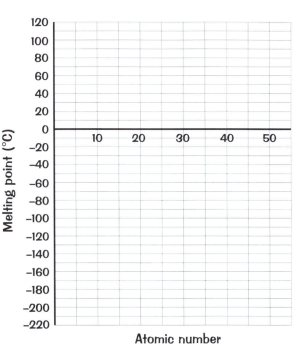

c) Explain fully why this relationship exists.

....

....

Giant Covalent Structures: Carbon

Q1   Circle the correct words to complete the following paragraph.

Giant covalent structures contain **charged ions** / **uncharged atoms**. The covalent bonds

between the atoms are **strong** / **weak**. Giant covalent structures have **high** / **low** melting

points and they are usually **soluble** / **insoluble** in water.

Q2   **Graphite** and **diamond** are both made entirely from **carbon**, but have different properties.

a)   Explain why graphite is a good conductor of electricity.

....

....

b)   Explain how diamond's structure makes it hard.

....

....

Q3   A molecule of **buckminsterfullerene** is made up of 60 carbon atoms.

a)   What is the **molecular formula** of buckminsterfullerene? ....

b)   How many covalent bonds does each carbon atom form? ....

c)   Can buckminsterfullerene conduct electricity? Explain your answer.

....

....

Q4   The different **forms** of carbon have different **properties** and **uses**.
From the list, select a suitable use for the following forms of carbon.
State the property that justifies your choice.

glass-cutting tool   **computer chips**   **pencils**

a)   **Fullerene nanotube** Use: ....

Property: ....

b)   **Graphite** Use: ....

Property: ....

c)   **Diamond** Use: ....

Property: ....

Treatment and Homeopathy

Q1 If you were conducting a **trial** of a new drug to test its effectiveness and safety, which of the following questions would you set out to answer? Tick one or more boxes.

A ☐ Do people like the taste of the drug?

B ☐ Do people get better after taking the drug?

C ☐ How much does the drug cost?

D ☐ Does the drug cause any serious side effects?

Taster, madam?

Q2 Draw lines to match the following terms to the sentence that best describes them.

Placebo

Homeopathic remedy

Control group

A highly diluted natural substance

A set of patients taking a placebo

A control 'medicine' which does not actually contain any drug

Q3 In order to test the **effectiveness** of a drug, a researcher gives the drug to a group of patients over a period of time and then carries out interviews to see if their condition has improved.

a) Why is this not a fair test of the drug?

....

b) Explain fully how you would improve the trial to make it a fair test.

....

....

....

c) What is meant by the 'placebo effect'?

....

....

Top Tips: Make sure you know all about placebos and drug testing — it's a vital part of making drugs (and answering exam questions). Homeopathic remedies are just as important here, too.

Treatment and Homeopathy

Q4 Homeopathic remedies are one type of alternative to conventional medicine.

a) Put the following stages in the preparation of a homeopathic remedy into the correct order.

   A The solution is diluted with water.   **B** The last two steps are repeated many times.

   C The solution is shaken.   **D** A chemical is extracted from a plant, animal or mineral.

   E The active ingredient is dissolved in alcohol.   **Order:** ....

b) What do homeopaths believe happens when the mixture is shaken?

   ....

c) Why don't homeopathic remedies have to go through the same testing process as other medicines?

   ....

d) Why do many scientists find it difficult to believe that homeopathic remedies really work?

   ....

   ....

Q5 In a **trial** designed to test the effectiveness of a **homeopathic cold remedy**, 100 people with a cold are given a drink. Fifty of the drinks contain the homeopathic remedy and fifty are **placebos**.

None of the volunteers know which they've been given. **Two days** later everyone is asked if they are feeling better. The results of the trial are summarised in the table.

Control group		Group taking remedy	
No. feeling better	No. not feeling better	No. feeling better	No. not feeling better
31	19	32	18

a) What percentage of the control group felt better after one week?

   ....

b) What percentage of the group taking the real remedy felt better after one week?

   ....

c) Suggest why some people in the control group (who took no remedy) felt better after one week.

   ....

d) Does the trial show that this remedy is effective? Explain your answer.

   ....

   ....

e) How could this trial be improved to give more reliable results?

   ....

Rates of Reaction

Q1   Circle the correct words to complete the statements below about **rates of reaction**.

a)   The higher the temperature, the faster / slower the rate of a reaction.

b)   A higher concentration will increase / reduce the rate of a reaction.

c)   If the reactants are gases / liquids, a higher pressure will give a faster / slower reaction.

d)   A larger particle size increases / decreases the rate of reaction.

e)   A catalyst speeds up / slows down the rate of reaction but is / isn't used up.

Q2   In an experiment, **different sizes** of marble chips were reacted with excess hydrochloric acid. The **same mass** of marble was used each time. The graph below shows how much **gas** was produced when using large marble chips (X), medium marble chips (Y) and small marble chips (Z).

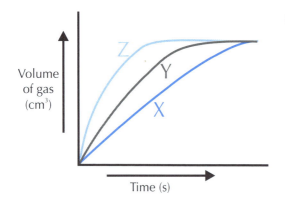

a)   i)   Which curve (X, Y or Z) shows the **fastest** reaction? Circle the correct answer.

X   Y   Z

ii) How can you tell this by looking at the graph?

....

....

....

b)   Why was an **excess** of acid used? ....

c)   Why do all the reactions produce the **same** volume of gas?

....

d)   On the graph, draw the curve you would expect to see if you used **more** of the small marble chips. Assume that all the other conditions are the same as before.

Q3   Another experiment investigated the **change in mass** of the reactants during a reaction in which a **gas** was given off. The graph below shows the results for three experiments carried out under different conditions.

a)   Suggest **why** reaction R involved a greater change in mass than reactions P and Q.

....

....

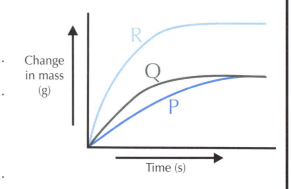

b)   What might have caused the difference between reaction P and reaction Q?

....

....

Measuring Rates of Reaction

Q1 Use the words provided to complete the sentences below about **measuring rates of reaction**.

faster   speed   volume   reactants   gas   mass   formed   precipitation

a) The .... of a reaction can be measured by observing either how quickly

the .... are used up or how quickly the products are ....

b) In a .... reaction you usually measure how quickly the product is formed.

The product turns the solution cloudy. The .... it turns cloudy the faster

the reaction.

c) In a reaction that produces a .... you can measure how quickly the

.... of the reactants changes or measure the .... of gas

given off in a certain time interval.

Q2 Sam conducted two experiments with equal masses of marble chips and equal volumes of hydrochloric acid (HCl). He used two **different concentrations** of acid and measured the **change in mass** of the reactants. Below is a graph of the results.

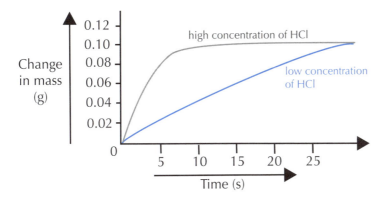

acid concentration

Circle the letter(s) to show the valid conclusion(s) you might draw **from this graph**.

A   Rate of reaction depends on the temperature of the reactants.

B   Increasing the concentration of the acid has no effect on the rate of reaction.

C   Rate of reaction depends on the acid concentration.

D   Rate of reaction depends on the mass of the marble chips.

Top Tips: It's a pretty good idea to learn the four things that reaction rate depends on, and it's not a bad idea to know the formula for calculating rate of reaction. Remember, graphs can be used to show reaction speeds, and there's also three methods of measuring reactions that you should know.

Measuring Rates of Reaction

Q3   Charlie was comparing the rate of reaction of 5 g of magnesium ribbon with 20 ml of **five different concentrations** of hydrochloric acid. Each time he measured how much **gas** was produced during the **first minute** of the reaction. He did the experiment **twice** for each concentration of acid and obtained these results:

Concentration of HCl (mol/dm³)	Experiment 1 — volume of gas produced (cm³)	Experiment 2 — volume of gas produced (cm³)	Average volume of gas produced (cm³)
2	92	96	
1.5	63	65	
1	44	47	
0.5	20	50	
0.25	9	9	

a)   Fill in the last column of the table.

b)   Circle the **anomalous** result in the table.

c)   Which concentration of hydrochloric acid produced the fastest rate of reaction? ....

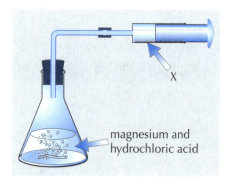

magnesium and hydrochloric acid

d)   A diagram of the **apparatus** used in the experiment is shown on the left.

    i)   What is the object marked **X** called?

    ....

    ii)   Name one other key piece of apparatus needed for this experiment (not shown in the diagram).

    ....

e)   **Sketch** a graph of the average volume of gas produced against concentration of HCl and **label** the axes. Do not include the anomalous result.

You don't need to plot the values, just draw what the graph would look like.

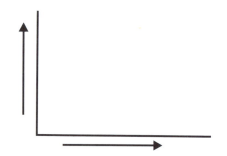

f)   Why did Charlie do the experiment twice and calculate the average volume?

....

g)   How might the anomalous result have come about?

....

h)   Suggest two changes Charlie could make to improve his results if he repeated his investigation.

1. ....

2. ....

Collision Theory

Q1   Circle the correct words to complete the sentences.

a)   In order for a reaction to occur, the particles must remain still / **collide**.

b)   If you heat up a reaction mixture, you give the particles more **energy** / surface area.

c)   This makes them move **faster** / more slowly and so there is **more** / less chance of successful collisions.

d)   So, increasing the temperature increases the concentration / **rate** of reaction.

Q2   Draw lines to match up the **changes** with their **effects**.

increasing the temperature

decreasing the concentration

adding a catalyst

increasing the surface area

provides a surface for particles to stick to and lowers activation energy

makes the particles move faster, so they collide more often

gives particles a bigger area of solid reactant to react with

means fewer particles of reactant are present, so fewer collisions occur

Q3   Gases are always under **pressure**.

a)   i)   If you increase the pressure on a gas reaction, does the rate of reaction **increase** or **decrease**?

....

ii)   Explain your answer. ....

....

....

b)   In the boxes on the right draw two diagrams — one showing particles of two different gases at low pressure, the other showing the same two gases at high pressure.

low pressure   high pressure

Q4   Here are four statements about **surface area** and **rates of reaction**. Tick the appropriate boxes to show whether they are true or false.

True   False

a)   Breaking a larger solid into smaller pieces decreases its surface area.

b)   A larger surface area means a faster rate of reaction.

c)   A larger surface area decreases the number of useful collisions.

d)   Powdered marble has a larger surface area than an equal mass of marble chips has.

Q5   Explain what a catalyst is and what it does.

....

....

Catalysts

Q1 To get a reaction to **start**, you have to give the particles some **energy**.

a) What is this energy called? Underline the correct answer.

potential energy   activation energy   chemical energy

b) The diagram opposite shows two reactions —
one with a catalyst and one without. Which
line shows the reaction **with** a catalyst? ....

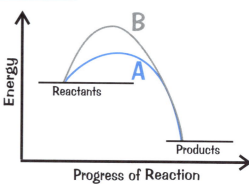

c) On this diagram, draw and label arrows to show the
activation energy for the reaction without a catalyst and
the activation energy for the reaction with a catalyst.

Q2 Solid catalysts come in **different forms**. Two examples are **pellets** and **fine gauze**.

Explain why solid catalysts are used in forms such as these.

....

....

Q3 Industrial catalysts are often **metals**.

You find them in the middle of the periodic table.

a) Which type of metal is commonly used? ....

b) Give an example of a metal catalyst and say which industrial process it is used in.

....

Q4 This question is about **enzymes**.

a) Underline **two** of the following descriptions that can be used to correctly describe an enzyme.

A A transition metal   **B** A biological catalyst   **C** A protein   **D** An element

b) Reactions in living organisms are catalysed by enzymes. Give two advantages of this.

....

....

c) Give the optimum temperature and pH for a **typical** human enzyme.

....

d) Explain what would happen to this enzyme if the temperature rose too far above the optimum.

....

....

Energy Transfer in Reactions

Q1 Use the words below to **complete** the blanks in the passage.

endothermic	exothermic	energy	heat	an increase	a decrease

All chemical reactions involve changes in ....

In .... reactions, ... energy is given out to the

surroundings. A thermometer will show .... in temperature.

In .... reactions, ... energy is taken in from the

surroundings. A thermometer will show .... in temperature.

Q2 Fiz investigated the **temperature change** during a reaction. She added 25 cm³ of sodium hydroxide solution to 25 cm³ of hydrochloric acid. She used a **data logger** to measure the temperature of the reaction over the first **five** seconds.

Fiz plotted her results on the graph shown.

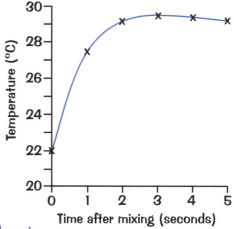

a) What was the increase in temperature due to the reaction?

....

b) Circle any of the words below that correctly describe the reaction in this experiment.

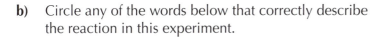

neutralisation   combustion   endothermic   respiration   exothermic

Q3 State whether bond **breaking** and bond **forming** are exothermic or endothermic reactions, and explain why in both cases.

Bond breaking ....

....

Bond forming ....

....

Q4 Decomposing 1 tonne (1000 kg) of CaCO₃ requires about 1 800 000 kJ of heat energy.

a) How much heat energy would be needed to make **1 kg** of CaCO₃ decompose?

....

b) How much CaCO₃ could be decomposed by **90 000 kJ** of heat energy?

....

Energy Transfer in Reactions

Q5 When **methane** burns in oxygen it forms carbon dioxide and water. The bonds in the methane and oxygen molecules **break** and new bonds are formed to make carbon dioxide and water molecules.

a) Is energy taken in or given out when the bonds in the methane and oxygen molecules break?

....

b) Is energy taken in or given out when the bonds in the carbon dioxide and water molecules form?

....

c) Methane is a fuel commonly used in cooking and heating. Do you think that burning methane is an exothermic or an endothermic process? Explain your answer.

....

....

d) Which of the following statements about burning methane is true? Circle one letter.

A **The energy involved in breaking bonds is greater than the energy involved in forming bonds.**

B **The energy involved in breaking bonds is less than the energy involved in forming bonds.**

C **The energy involved in breaking bonds is the same as the energy involved in forming bonds.**

Q6 Here are some practical uses of chemical reactions. Decide whether each reaction is **endothermic** or **exothermic**. In the box, put **N** for endothermic and **X** for exothermic.

a) A camping stove burns methylated spirit to heat a pan of beans. ☐

b) Special chemical cool packs are used by athletes to treat injuries. They are placed on the skin and draw heat away from the injury. ☐

c) Self-heating cans of coffee contain chemicals in the base. When the chemicals are combined they produce heat which warms the can. ☐

d) Baking powder is used to make cakes rise. When it's heated in the oven it thermally decomposes to produce a gas. ☐

Top Tips: Anything that takes heat in is **endothermic**. Endothermic reactions are not unusual in everyday life — think about what happens when you cook eggs and use baking powder.

Reversible Reactions

Q1   Use words from the list below to complete the following sentences about **reversible reactions**.

escape   reactants   catalysts   closed   products   react   balance

a)   In a reversible reaction, the .... of the reaction can themselves

.... to give the original ....

b)   At equilibrium, the amounts of reactants and products reach a ....

c)   To reach equilibrium the reaction must happen in a .... system,

where products and reactants can't ....

Q2   Look at this diagram of a **reversible reaction**.

a)   For the forward reaction:

   i)   give the reactant(s)   ....

   ii)   give the product(s)   ....

b)   Here are two labels:

| **X** product splits up |
| **Y** reactants combine |

The reaction going from left to right is called the forward reaction. The reaction going from right to left is called the backward reaction.

   i)   Which of these labels goes in position 1 — X or Y?   ....

   ii)   Which goes in position 2 — X or Y?   ....

c)   Write the equation for the reversible reaction.   ....

d)   Complete the sentence by circling the correct phrase.

In a dynamic equilibrium, the forward and backward reactions are happening:

at different rates / at zero rate / at the same rate.

Q3   Which of these statements about reversible reactions are **true** and which are **false**?

	True	**False**
a) The position of an equilibrium depends on the reaction conditions.	☐	☐
b) Upon reaching a dynamic equilibrium, the reactions stop taking place.	☐	☐
c) You can move the position of equilibrium to get more product.	☐	☐
d) At equilibrium there will always be equal quantities of products and reactants.	☐	☐

Reversible Reactions

Q4 Substances A and B react to produce substances C and D in a **reversible reaction**.

$$2A_{(g)} + B_{(g)} \rightleftharpoons 2C_{(g)} + D_{(g)}$$

a) Give two reaction conditions which often affect the **position of equilibrium**.

1. .... 2. ....

b) The forward reaction is **exothermic**. Does the backward reaction give out or take in heat? Explain your answer.

....

....

c) If the temperature is raised, does the **forward** or **backward** reaction increase? ....

d) Explain why changing the temperature of a reversible reaction always affects the position of the equilibrium.

....

e) What effect will changing the **pressure** have on the position of equilibrium in this reaction? Explain your answer.

....

Q5 Look at the equation showing another **reversible reaction** below.

a) In this reaction:
$$2SO_{2(g)} + O_{2(g)} \rightleftharpoons 2SO_{3(g)}$$

i) Which reaction, forward or backward, is accompanied by a **decrease** in volume? Explain your answer.

....

ii) How will increasing the pressure affect the position of equilibrium in this reaction?

....

b) What does adding a catalyst to a reversible reaction do?
Circle the letter next to the correct answer.

    A   It moves the equilibrium position towards the products.

    B   It makes the reaction reach equilibrium more quickly.

    C   It moves the equilibrium position towards the reactants.

    D   It causes a decrease in pressure.

c) What happens to the amount of product at equilibrium when you use a catalyst?

....

The Haber Process

Q1 The Haber process is used to make **ammonia**. The equation for the reaction is:

$$N_2(g) + 3H_2(g) \rightleftharpoons 2NH_3(g)$$

a) Name the reactants in the forward reaction. ....

b) Which side of the equation has more molecules? ....

c) How should the pressure be changed in order to produce more ammonia? Explain your answer.

....

Q2 The **industrial conditions** for the Haber process are carefully chosen.

a) What conditions are used? Tick one box.

☐ **1000 atmospheres, 450 °C**　☐ **200 atmospheres, 1000 °C**　☐ **450 atmospheres, 200 °C**　☐ **200 atmospheres, 450 °C**

b) Give two reasons why the pressure used is chosen.

1. ....

2. ....

Q3 In the Haber process reaction, the **forward** reaction is **exothermic**.

a) What effect will raising the temperature have on the **amount** of ammonia formed?

....

b) Explain why a high temperature is used industrially.

....

c) What happens to the leftover nitrogen and hydrogen? ....

Q4 **Ammonium nitrate** is used by farmers as a fertiliser.

a) Fill in the blanks to show the reactants used to produce ammonium nitrate.

.... + ... → ammonium nitrate

b) Explain why it makes a good fertiliser. ....

....

c) Give **one advantage** and **one disadvantage** of using artificial fertilisers like ammonium nitrate in farming, rather then using organic alternatives.

....

....

....

Mixed Questions — C2 Topics 7 & 8

Q1 The bonding and electron arrangement in a molecule of **silane**, SiH_4, is similar to that in **methane**.

a) What type of bonding is present in methane?

....

b) Draw a diagram to show the electron arrangement in **silane** in the box provided.

Q2 **Iodine** exists as simple **diatomic molecules**, I_2.

a) Explain why iodine has a low melting point. ....

....

b) Predict whether iodine is likely to be able to conduct electricity. Justify your prediction.

....

c) Why do the melting and boiling points of the halogens increase as you go down the group?

....

....

Q3 The following questions concern three forms of **carbon** — **diamond**, **graphite** and **buckminsterfullerene**. Diamond's melting point is 3550 °C and graphite's is 3652 °C.

a) Explain why graphite and diamond have very high melting points.

....

....

b) Explain why buckminsterfullerene and graphite conduct electricity, but diamond does not.

....

....

Q4 **Homeopathic remedies** contain diluted doses of natural substances that produce symptoms of illness. However, unlike conventional medicines, they do **not** have to be rigorously tested.

a) Explain why this is. ....

....

b) People who take homeopathic medicines often feel better, even though there is little scientific evidence that the medicine itself has any physical effect. Suggest a **scientific** explanation for this.

....

<u>Mixed Questions — C2 Topics 7 & 8</u>

Q5 The results of a reaction between **calcium carbonate** and **hydrochloric acid** are shown on the graph.

a) The products of this reaction are calcium chloride (which forms a colourless solution), water and carbon dioxide. Suggest how the rate of this reaction could be measured.

....

....

b) Which part of the curve shows the fastest rate of reaction — A, B or C? ....

c) Explain what happens to the reaction at point C.

....

d) At 35 °C, the reaction followed the curve shown on the graph. Draw two other curves on the same diagram to show how the rate of reaction might change at 25 °C and 45 °C.

e) Give three factors other than temperature on which the rate of reaction depends.

....

Q6 **Ammonium nitrate** is an artificial fertiliser formed from a reaction between ammonia and nitric acid.

a) Outline the environmental and health problems that may be caused by widespread use of ammonium nitrate.

....

....

....

b) What can farmers do to help avoid these problems?

....

Q7 In many reactions, a **catalyst** can be used to increase the **reaction rate**.

a) Explain how a catalyst works.

....

....

b) Which form would be better as a catalyst, a stick or a powder? Explain your answer.

....

....

Mixed Questions — C2 Topics 7 & 8

Q8   **Iodine** vapour reacts with **hydrogen** to form hydrogen iodide.
The reaction is **endothermic** and the mixture turns from purple to colourless.

$$I - I \ + \ H - H \longrightarrow 2(H - I)$$

a)   Which old bonds are broken?   ....

b)   Which new bonds are made?   ....

c)   Which of the processes is endothermic — breaking bonds or forming new ones?

....

d)   Do you think that the temperature of the reaction vessel will rise or fall during this reaction?
Explain your answer.

....

e)   What effect does lowering the activation energy (by using a catalyst) have on a reaction?

....

Q9   The **thermal decomposition** of ammonium chloride is a **reversible reaction**.

$$NH_4Cl\,(s) \ \underset{\text{exothermic}}{\overset{\text{endothermic}}{\rightleftharpoons}} \ NH_3\,(g) \ + \ HCl\,(g)$$

a)   In which direction will the equilibrium move if the temperature is increased?

....

b)   In which direction will the equilibrium move if the pressure is increased?

....

Q10   The rate of a chemical reaction can be **increased** by using a **catalyst** or increasing the **temperature**.

a)   What catalyst is used in the Haber process?

....

b)   The Haber process takes place at a temperature of 450 °C. By considering the effect on the yield
and the rate of reaction, explain why a catalyst is used rather than using a higher temperature.

....

....

....

Analysing Substances

Q1   Use the words to complete the passage.

method	only	quantitative	sample	qualitative	much

The first stage in any analysis is to choose the most suitable analytical

.... A .... method can be used if you

.... want to find out what substances are present in a

...................................., but if you want to find out how ....

of each substance is present then a .... analysis is necessary.

Q2   Explain why it might be important to know:

a)   the concentration of **chlorine** in a swimming pool ....

....

b)   the concentration of **alcohol** in blood ....

....

c)   the **nitrate ion** concentration in drinking water ....

....

Q3   Maria was asked to identify the **solute** present in a sample of water.
It was known to be a single ionic compound.

Step 1 — Maria took 5 cm³ of the water and added a small quantity of sodium hydroxide solution.
A **white precipitate** was formed that dissolved when more of the alkali was added. This told Maria
that the **aluminium ion** was present.

Step 2 — Maria took a further 25 cm³ of water and added some dilute hydrochloric acid followed by
an excess of barium chloride solution. A **white precipitate** was formed showing Maria that the
sulphate ion was present.

a)   Circle the correct answer for each of the following questions.

i)   What sort of analysis is carried out in Step 1 of the procedure?   qualitative / quantitative

ii) What sort of analysis is carried out in Step 2 of the procedure?   qualitative / quantitative

b)   What must be the identity of the mystery solute? ....

Top Tips: Chemical analysis isn't just for forensic scientists — it's important in chemistry too.
Make sure you know what qualitative and quantitative analyses are, and be ready to explain how you'd
identify ionic compounds — remember you have to test for both the positive and the negative ion.

Tests for Positive Ions

Q1   Robert adds a solution of **sodium hydroxide** to a solution of
calcium chloride. The formula of the calcium ion is Ca^{2+}.

a)   What would Robert observe?

   ....

b)   Write the balanced symbol equation for the reaction, including state symbols.

   ....

c)   Write the balanced **ionic equation** for this reaction, including state symbols.

   ....

Q2   Les had four samples of **metal compounds**. He tested each one by placing a small amount on the
end of a wire and putting it into a Bunsen flame. He observed the **colour of flame** produced.

a)   Draw lines to match each of Les's observations to the metal cation producing the coloured flame.

brick-red flame	Na^+
yellow/orange flame	Cu^{2+}
blue-green flame	K^+
lilac flame	Ca^{2+}

b)   Les wants to make a firework which will explode in his local football team's colour, **lilac**.
Which of the following compounds should he use? Circle your answer.

silver nitrate   sodium chloride   barium sulphate   potassium nitrate   calcium carbonate

Q3   Cilla adds a few drops of **NaOH** solution to
solutions of different **metal compounds**.

Metal Cation	Colour of Precipitate
Fe^{2+}	
	blue
Fe^{3+}	
Al^{3+}	

a)   Complete her table of results.

b)   Complete the balanced ionic equation for the reaction of iron(II) ions with hydroxide ions.

   $Fe^{2+}($........$)$ + ... $OH^-(aq)$ → .... (s)

c)   Write a balanced ionic equation for the reaction of **iron(III) ions** with hydroxide ions.   *Don't forget state symbols.*

   ....

d)   Cilla adds a few drops of sodium hydroxide solution to **aluminium sulphate solution**.
She continues adding sodium hydroxide to excess. What would she observe at each stage?

   ....

   ....

Tests for Positive Ions

Q4 Claire was given a solid sample of a mixture of two ionic compounds. She was told that they were thought to be **ammonium chloride** and **calcium chloride**.

a) Describe, in detail, how she would test for the presence of the two **positive ions**.

....

....

....

b) What would she **observe** at each stage?

....

....

c) Write **ionic equations** for the reactions that identify the positive ions.

....

....

Q5 Select compounds from the box to match the following statements.

KCl	LiCl	$FeSO_4$	NH_4Cl	$FeCl_3$	$Al_2(SO_4)_3$
NaCl	$CuSO_4$	$CaCl_2$	$MgCl_2$	$BaCl_2$	

a) This compound forms a blue precipitate with sodium hydroxide solution. ....

b) This compound forms a white precipitate with sodium hydroxide that dissolves if excess sodium hydroxide is added. ....

c) This compound forms a green precipitate with sodium hydroxide solution. ....

d) This compound forms a reddish brown precipitate with sodium hydroxide solution. ....

e) This compound reacts with sodium hydroxide to release a pungent gas. ....

f) This compound reacts with sodium hydroxide to form a white precipitate, and it also gives a brick-red flame in a flame test. ....

Top Tips: Right, this stuff needs to be learnt properly. Otherwise you'll be stuck in your exam staring at a question about the colour that some random solution goes when you add something you've never heard of before to it, and all you'll know is that ammonia smells of cat wee.

Tests for Negative Ions

Q1 Give the chemical formulae of the **negative ions** present in the following compounds.

a) barium sulphate .... **b)** potassium iodide .... **c)** silver bromide ....

Q2 Choose from the words given to complete the passage below.

carbon dioxide	limewater	hydrochloric acid	sodium hydroxide	hydrogen

A test for the presence of carbonates in an unidentified substance involves reacting it with dilute .... If carbonates are present then .... will be formed. You can test for this by bubbling it through .... to see if it becomes milky.

Q3 Answer the following questions on testing for **sulphate** and **sulphite** ions.

a) Which two **chemicals** are used to test for sulphate ions?

....

b) What would you **see** after adding these chemicals to a sulphate compound?

....

c) **i)** What substance is used to test for sulphite ions? ....

ii) Describe what you would see after adding this substance to a sulphite compound.

....

....

Q4 Deirdre wants to find out if a soluble compound contains **chloride**, **bromide** or **iodide** ions. Explain how she could do this.

....

....

....

Q5 Complete the following symbol equations for reactions involved in **tests for negative ions**.

a) $Ag^+(aq) +$ .... $\rightarrow AgCl(s)$

b) $2HCl(aq) + Na_2CO_3(s) \rightarrow 2NaCl(aq) +$ ....(l) + ...(g)

c) .... + ... $\rightarrow BaSO_4(s)$

Tests for Acids and Alkalis

Q1 Acids and alkalis can be tested for using indicators.

a) Complete the following statement about litmus indicator with the correct colours.

Acids turn .... litmus ...., and alkalis turn .... litmus ....

b) Which ions are always present in an acid? ....

c) How would you test for the presence of an acid other than using an indicator?
Describe the result of this test if an acid is present.

....

....

....

d) Which ions are always present in an alkali? ....

e) Other than using an indicator, how would you test for the presence of an alkali?
Describe the result of this test if an alkali is present.

....

....

....

Q2 Ammonia gas can be prepared in the laboratory by heating solid ammonium chloride with solid **calcium hydroxide**.

a) Write a balanced **symbol equation** for this preparation of ammonia.

....

b) Write the **ionic equation** for this reaction.

....

c) Describe how you could test for ammonia.

....

d) What colour will a solution of calcium hydroxide be with **phenolphthalein**?

....

Top Tips: Acids and alkalis is important stuff — and being able to explain how you'd identify H^+ and OH^- ions is a big indicator (ha ha) to the examiners of how much you know. So get learning...

Measuring Amounts — Moles

Q1 a) **Complete** the following sentence.

> One mole of atoms or molecules of any substance will have a .... in grams
> equal to the .... for that substance.

b) What is the **mass** of each of the following?

i) 1 mole of copper ....

ii) 3 moles of chlorine **gas** ....

iii) 2 moles of nitric acid (HNO_3) ....

iv) 0.5 moles of calcium carbonate ($CaCO_3$) ....

Q2 a) Write down the formula for calculating the **number of moles in a given mass**.

....

b) How many **moles** are there in each of the following?

i) 20 g of calcium ....

ii) 112 g of sulphur ....

iii) 200 g of copper oxide (CuO) ....

c) Calculate the **mass** of each of the following.

i) 2 moles of sodium ....

ii) 0.75 moles of magnesium oxide (MgO) ....

iii) 0.025 moles of lead chloride ($PbCl_2$) ....

Q3 Ali adds **13 g** of zinc to **50 cm³** of hydrochloric acid. All of the zinc reacts.

$$Zn + 2HCl \rightarrow ZnCl_2 + H_2$$

a) How many moles of **zinc** were added?

Look at the
symbol equation.

....

b) How many moles of **hydrochloric acid** reacted?

....

Measuring Amounts — Moles

Q4   Jenni added some **magnesium carbonate** to an excess of **dilute sulphuric acid**. A reaction occurred which produced 3 g of magnesium sulphate and some carbon dioxide gas.

  a)   Write a balanced **symbol equation** for the reaction.

....

  b)   What mass of **magnesium carbonate** did Jenni add to the acid?

....

....

  c)   What mass of **sulphuric acid** was used up in the reaction?

....

....

  d)   What mass of **carbon dioxide** was produced?

....

....

Q5   Dr Burette adds **0.6 g** of sodium to water. Sodium hydroxide and hydrogen form. (All the sodium reacts.)

  a)   Write a **balanced symbol equation** for this reaction.

....

  b)   What mass of **hydrogen** is produced?

....

....

  c)   Calculate the mass of **sodium hydroxide** produced.

....

....

Top Tips: So, you already know that the mole is not just a small burrowing animal. Now you need to make sure that you can convert between moles and grams. But that's not all — make sure you learn the formula for calculating the number of moles and you'll soon be sailing through those exam questions.

C3 Topic 3 — Chemical Detection

Calculating Volumes

Q1 Choose from the following words to complete the passage.

atmosphere	decreased	volume	26	higher
mass	increased	25	vole	mole	24

One .... of any gas will always occupy .... dm³ when the

.... is measured at a temperature of .... °C and a pressure of

1 .... If the volume is measured at a .... temperature, the molar

volume of gas is increased. If the pressure is ...., the molar volume decreases.

Q2 The **limewater test** for carbon dioxide involves the reaction between carbon dioxide and calcium hydroxide, which is shown in the following equation:

$$CO_2 + Ca(OH)_2 \rightarrow CaCO_3 + H_2O$$

A solution of limewater containing 0.37 g of calcium hydroxide reacts with carbon dioxide at RTP.

a) What mass of **carbon dioxide** is needed to react completely with the limewater?

....

b) What **volume** does this amount of carbon dioxide occupy at RTP?

....

Q3 Methane burns in oxygen to produce carbon dioxide and water.

3.2 g of methane was completely burned in oxygen and the volume of each gas was measured. This was carried out at 112 °C and 1 atmosphere pressure. (1 mole of gas occupies 31 dm³ at 112 °C and 1 atmosphere pressure.)

a) Write a balanced **equation** for the reaction.

....

b) What volume of **methane** was used in the reaction?

....

c) How much **oxygen** (in dm³) reacted with the methane?

....

d) Calculate the **total volume of products** formed in this reaction.

Don't forget that water is a gas at temperatures above 100 °C.

....

....

C3 Topic 3 — Chemical Detection

Quantitative Chemistry and Solutions

Q1 Complete the table. ➡️

MOLES	VOLUME	CONCENTRATION (moles/dm³)
2	4 dm³	a)
0.5	2 dm³	b)
0.2	500 cm³	c)
0.2	100 cm³	d)

Q2 Work out how many **moles** of sodium hydroxide there are in:

a) 2 dm³ of a 0.5 M sodium hydroxide solution.

b) 100 cm³ of a 0.1 M sodium hydroxide solution.

Q3 Convert the solution concentrations below from **moles/dm³** to **g/dm³**.

a) 2 mol/dm³ sodium hydroxide, NaOH.

How many moles?

b) 0.1 mol/dm³ glucose, $C_6H_{12}O_6$.

Q4 Susan wants to work out the concentration of a solution of sodium chloride. She puts 5 ml of the solution in a pre-weighed, clean, dry evaporating basin and heats the basin until all the water appears to have evaporated.

a) What would Susan do next? Explain why she would do this.

b) After doing this, how can she calculate the mass of sodium chloride that was dissolved?

Q5 **10 cm³** of potassium chloride solution was heated gently to evaporate all the water. The mass of the basin and dry potassium chloride was **50.400 g**. (The mass of the basin when empty was 49.655 g.)

Calculate:

a) The **mass concentration** of the solution of potassium chloride.

b) The **molar concentration** of the solution of potassium chloride.

Titrations

Q1   Work out the number of **moles** in the following solutions.

  a)   1 dm³ of 2 mol/dm³ HCl.

....

  b)   100 cm³ of 1 mol/dm³ NaOH.

....

  c)   25 cm³ of 0.1 mol/dm³ HNO₃.

....

  d)   10 cm³ of 0.2 mol/dm³ Ca(OH)₂.

....

Q2   Circle the answer which best completes each of these sentences.

  a)   During acid/alkali titrations...

   ...methyl orange is always a suitable indicator.   ...the alkali must always go in the burette.

   ...the tap is opened fully near the end of the titration.   ...the flask is swirled regularly.

  b)   Phenolphthalein was added to sodium hydroxide in a flask as part of a titration with an acid.
       The indicator colour change at the end-point of the titration was...

   ...yellow/orange to red.   ...red to yellow/orange.

   ...colourless to pink.   ...pink to colourless.

Q3   A **titration** procedure was used to compare the **acid concentration** of some
       fizzy drinks. The acids present included carbonic, citric and ethanoic.

  a)   Name the **independent variable** and the **dependent variable** in this experiment.

       Independent variable: ....

       Dependent variable: ....

  b)   Suggest a suitable **indicator** and describe the **colour change** which would occur.

       ....

       The titration values (titres) are shown in the table below.

fizzy drink	1st titre (cm³)	2nd titre (cm³)
Fizzade	15.2	14.6
Kolafizz	20.5	19.8
Cherriade	12.6	12.1

  c)   Which drink contained the most acid?

       ....

C3 Topic 3 — Chemical Detection

Titrations

Q4 The concentration of some limewater, **Ca(OH)$_2$,** was determined by titration with hydrochloric acid, **HCl. 50 cm^3** of limewater required **20 cm^3** of **0.1 mol/dm^3** hydrochloric acid to neutralise it. Work out the concentration of the limewater in **g/dm^3** using the steps outlined below.

a) How many moles of HCl are present in 20 cm^3 of 0.1 mol/dm^3 solution?

....

b) Complete the equation for the reaction.

.... + ... → CaCl$_2$ + ...

c) From the equation, ... mole(s) of HCl reacts with .... mole(s) of Ca(OH)$_2$.

d) Use your answers to a) and c) to work out how many moles of Ca(OH)$_2$ there are in 50 cm^3 of limewater.

....

e) What is the concentration of the limewater in **moles per dm^3**?

....

f) What is the concentration of the limewater in **grams per dm^3**?

....

Q5 In a titration, **10 cm^3** of sulphuric acid was used to neutralise **30 cm^3** of **0.1 mol/dm^3** potassium hydroxide solution**.**

$$H_2SO_4 + 2KOH \rightarrow K_2SO_4 + 2H_2O$$

a) What was the concentration of the sulphuric acid in **moles per dm^3**?

....

....

....

....

....

b) What is the concentration of the sulphuric acid in **grams per dm^3**?

....

....

Top Tips:
Aargh, not calculations... As if Chemistry wasn't tricky enough without some maths getting involved too (but at least it's not as bad as Physics). Actually, these aren't the worst calculations — as long as you remember to tackle them in stages and you know your equations.

Water

Q1 Suggest two ways in which water is used in each of the following places.

a) In the home ....

b) In agriculture ....

c) In industry ....

Q2 Indicate whether the following statements are true or false.

		True	False
a)	Water dissolves many ionic compounds.	☐	☐
b)	Water dissolves many covalent compounds.	☐	☐
c)	Sugars, salts and amino acids are transported around the body in solution in water.	☐	☐
d)	Many diseases, like cholera, are carried by microorganisms in water.	☐	☐

Q3 Answer the questions about water.

a) Why is water called the **universal solvent**?

....

b) How does water dissolve an **ionic** compound?

....

....

c) Why is water essential for **life**?

....

....

d) Why are many **power stations** situated next to rivers? ....

....

e) Why is it important not to **waste** water?

....

....

Top Tips: Water has lots of everyday uses that we take for granted — make sure you can list some of these. You also need to know the importance of purifying water and not wasting it.

Water

Q4   Read the passage about water and answer the questions that follow.

> All sorts of substances get mixed with tap water. They include shampoo, toothpaste, washing powder and detergents, grease, body waste, sand and various waste from factories. All this goes down the plug hole into the drains and becomes known as sewage. The sewage flows through underground pipes to a sewage plant, where the water in it is cleaned up and put back into the river or water supply.
>
> The sewage is first pumped through a screen to remove any rags, paper and large debris. It goes into settling tanks where most of the solids sink to the bottom. Chemicals are then added to make all the smaller particles stick together. The clean water is taken off the top and put into the river. The sludge that remains is treated with special bacteria that break down the harmful compounds. The digested sludge is either put in landfill sites, burned to produce energy or put on the land as fertiliser. Not many years ago, all the sludge would have been dumped in the sea.

a)   What activities in the **home** would put substances into sewage?

....

b)   Why are chemicals added to the **settling tanks**?

....

c)   Give one advantage and one disadvantage of **burning digested sludge**.

....

....

d)   Give one advantage and one disadvantage of putting sludge in **landfill**.

....

....

Q5   Water needs to be very pure for **drinking** and for use in **power station boilers**.

a)   Explain why water used in power stations boilers needs to be very pure.

....

....

b)   Give **three** things that are carried out at water treatment works to make the water purer.

....

....

Mixed Questions — C3 Topic 3

Q1   Sam is taking part in a chemistry competition where she needs to be able to identify various **ions**.

a)   Sam has a flowchart to help her identify **halide ions** present in a water sample.
Complete the gaps in her flowchart.

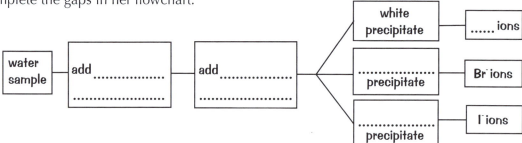

b)   What type of analysis would this be? ....

c)   Sam has another flowchart for identifying **positive ions**.
Fill in the gaps.

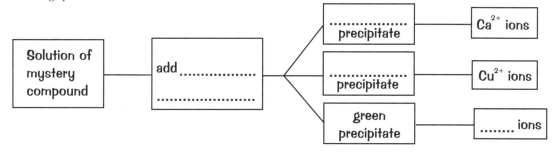

d)   Sam knows that if she adds sodium hydroxide solution to a solution of aluminium ions, there will
be a white precipitate which will then redissolve in excess sodium hydroxide to form a colourless
solution. Write the ionic equations including state symbols for these two reactions.

....

....

e)   Sam wants to test for H^+ ions in a solution. Describe how she could do this.

....

....

f)   Describe how Sam could test for the presence of SO_3^{2-} ions in a substance.

....

....

g)   Why will water dissolve many of the ionic compounds that Sam tests?

....

....

Mixed Questions — C3 Topic 3

Q2 Magnesium reacts with nitric acid, HNO_3, to form **magnesium nitrate**, $Mg(NO_3)_2$, and hydrogen.

a) Work out the relative formula mass of magnesium nitrate.

....

b) When 0.12 g of magnesium reacted with excess acid, 0.74 g of magnesium nitrate was formed.

   i) Calculate the number of moles of magnesium that reacted and the number of moles of magnesium nitrate produced.

....

....

   ii) The total volume of the solution formed was 0.2 dm^3. Work out the concentration of magnesium nitrate in this solution using your answer from part i).

....

   iii) If 0.025 moles of nitric acid was used, what mass of nitric acid was this?

....

   iv) Calculate the volume of hydrogen produced in the reaction (at RTP).

....

....

....

Q3 Jim carried out a **titration** as part of his chemistry coursework.

a) In his titration, Jim used 20 cm^3 of sulphuric acid to neutralise 35 cm^3 of 0.1 M sodium hydroxide solution. Find the concentration of the acid.

....

....

....

....

b) Suggest an indicator which Jim could have used during his titration, and give the colours it would be in acidic and alkaline solutions.

Indicator: ....

Acidic solution: ....

Alkaline solution: ....

Transition Elements

Q1 Complete the passage below by circling the correct word(s) from each pair.

> Most metals are in the transition block found **at the left** / **in the middle** of the periodic table.
> The transition metals are usually **reactive** / **unreactive** with oxygen and water. They generally
> have high **densities** / **volatilities** and **low** / **high** melting points. They are **good** / **poor**
> conductors of heat and electricity. Their compounds are often **coloured** / **shiny** and, like the
> metals themselves, are effective **fuels** / **catalysts** in many reactions.

Q2 Circle the correct answer for each of the following questions.

  a) Which one of the following properties applies to **all metals**?

   high density   good conductivity   high tensile strength

  b) Which one of the following properties applies to **all transition metals**?

   high melting point   poor conductivity   colourful

  c) Which property of most transition metals makes them useful as **pigments** and **dyes**?

   colourful compounds   high melting point   shiny appearance

Q3 Transition metals and their compounds often make **good catalysts**.

Draw lines to match the metals and compounds below to the reactions they catalyse.

iron

manganese(IV) oxide

nickel

vanadium pentoxide

converting natural oils into fats

ammonia production

decomposition of hydrogen peroxide

sulphuric acid production

Q4 'Chemical gardens' can be made by sprinkling **transition metal salts** into **sodium silicate solution**. Transition metal silicate crystals grow upwards as shown.

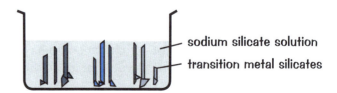

sodium silicate solution
transition metal silicates

Circle the three colours that you would be likely to see in the garden if potassium chromate(VI), potassium manganate(VII) and copper(II) sulphate crystals are used.

   red   orange   yellow   green   blue   purple

Transition Elements

Q5 Draw lines to connect the correct phrases in each column.
One has been done for you.

Metal / Alloy	Other Elements	Use
low-carbon steel	nothing	blades for tools
iron from a blast furnace	chromium	cutlery
high-carbon steel	0.1% carbon	car bodies
stainless steel	1.5% carbon	ornamental railings

Q6 Copper is commonly used in **electrical wires** and **plumbing**.

a) Give three properties of copper that are **typical** of transition elements.

....

b) Give another property that makes it ideal for use in:

i) electrical wiring ....

ii) plumbing ....

Q7 Read the description of **metal X** and answer the question that follows.

> Metal **X** is found in the block of elements between Group 2 and 3
> of the periodic table. It has a melting point of 1860 °C and a
> density of 7.2 g/cm³. The metal is used to provide the attractive
> coating on most motorbikes and bathroom taps. The metal forms
> two coloured chlorides, XCl_2 (blue) and XCl_3 (green).

Identify five pieces of evidence in the passage which suggest that metal X is a transition metal.

1. ....

2. ....

3. ....

4. ....

5. ....

Alcohols

Q1 Alcohols are a common group of chemicals.

a) What is the general formula of an alcohol? ....

b) Complete the following table.

Alcohol	No. of Carbon Atoms	Molecular Formula	Displayed Formula
Methanol			
	2		
		C_3H_7OH	
			H H H H | | | | H–C–C–C–C–O–H | | | H H H
	5		

Q2 The molecular formula for **ethanol** can be written as C_2H_5OH or as C_2H_6O.

a) What is the functional group found in all alcohols? ....

b) Explain why it is better to write ethanol's formula as C_2H_5OH.

....

Q3 Complete the following passage using the words below.

fuel	diesel	non-renewable	fermentation	lubricant	land
more	renewable	oxidation	sunshine	petrol	less

Ethanol can be mixed with .... and used as a .... for

cars. The more ethanol used in the mixture, the .... pollution

produced. In some countries ethanol is made by the .... of plants

such as sugar cane. Making ethanol this way uses a natural and ....

resource. The sugar cane can be grown continuously, but you need plenty of

.... and ....

Alcohols

Q4 Tick the correct boxes to show whether the following statements are **true** or **false**. **True False**

a) Ethanol is a clear, colourless liquid at room temperature.

b) Methanol is a non-volatile alcohol.

c) Propanol is miscible with water.

d) Alcohols burn to produce sulphur dioxide and water.

e) Alcohols can react with oxygen to produce carboxylic acids.

f) Alcohols can react with carboxylic acids to produce alkanes.

g) Methanol is less toxic than ethanol.

Q5 **Ethanol** is commonly used as a **solvent**.

a) Which part of ethanol's structure allows it to dissolve substances like hydrocarbons, oils and fats?

....

b) Which part of ethanol's structure allows it to mix with water and dissolve ionic compounds?

....

c) Ethanol is used in such things as glues, varnishes, printing inks, paints, deodorants and aftershaves. Give **two** properties of ethanol that often make it a good choice as a solvent.

....

Hint — these products need to 'dry'.

d) **Meths** is ethanol with other chemicals added to it. Give two of the other chemicals and explain why they're added.

1. ....

2. ....

Q6 Name the alcohol described in the passage below.

When alcohols react with oxygen they don't lose any of their carbon atoms.

> The alcohol is a clear colourless liquid that is **volatile**. It is completely **miscible** with water. When it reacts with oxygen it produces a carboxylic acid with **3 carbon atoms**.

Alcohol = ...

Top Tips: You need to know the **structures**, **formulae**, **physical properties** and the **uses** of alcohols. And I don't just mean in the production of alcoholic drinks. There are lots of other potentially far more useful things you can do with alcohol — like using it as a fuel in cars (but I wouldn't suggest tipping your dad's favourite whisky into his car — he probably won't be best pleased).

Carboxylic Acids

Q1 Tick the correct boxes to show whether the following statements are **true** or **false**.

True False

a) Carboxylic acids have the functional group –COOH.

b) There are six carbon atoms in every molecule of propanoic acid.

c) The longer the hydrocarbon chain, the less soluble a carboxylic acid is in water.

d) Ethanoic acid reacts with sodium hydroxide to produce sodium ethanoate and water.

Q2 Match up the following carboxylic acids to the correct statement.

Methanoic acid...

Citric acid...

Ethanoic acid...

Butanoic acid...

...has four carbon atoms in every molecule.

...is produced when beer is left in the open air.

...has the displayed formula $H-C{\overset{O}{\underset{O-H}{}}}$

...is used as a descaler.

Q3 Use the words given to complete the passage about everyday **carboxylic acids**.

| fatty | regular | detergents | aspirin | blood | preservative | cheese |
| attacks | chubby | rayon | relief | nylon | oranges | vinegar |

Carboxylic acids are an important part of several substances used in the home. Ethanoic acid is found in ...., which is not only used as a .... and flavouring, but is also used in the manufacture of the clothing fibre, ... Citric acid is present in fruits like .... and lemons and is used in fizzy drinks. .... is widely used for pain .... and has been shown to reduce .... clotting. Many people at risk of heart .... take aspirin on a .... basis. Longer chain carboxylic acids are commonly called .... acids and are used in ....

Q4 **Ethanoic acid** reacts with **calcium** like any other acid would.

a) Write the word equation for this reaction.

....

b) Write the balanced symbol equation for this reaction.

....

c) Suggest two safety precautions that should be taken when handling carboxylic acids.

....

Esters

Q1 Complete the sentences below by circling the correct word from each pair.

a) The fruit flavours used in some sweets are made by mixing man-made **esters** / **alcohols** together.

b) Esters **do** / **don't** mix very well with water, and **do** / **don't** mix well with alcohols.

c) Most esters are colourless **gases** / **liquids**.

d) Esters **are** / **aren't** volatile.

e) Many esters are highly **unreactive** / **flammable**, which can lead to a flash **fire** / **flood**.

Q2 Name the **ester** formed from the following combinations of **alcohols** and **carboxylic acids**.

a) ethanol + methanoic acid ....

b) methanol + propanoic acid ....

c) propanol + ethanoic acid ....

Ha ha ha - snort - ha ha ha haaa! You're giving me esterics!

Q3 **Methanol** reacts with **propanoic acid** to produce **methyl propanoate** and water.

a) Draw the displayed formula equation for this reaction in the space below.

b) Name a catalyst that can be used in this reaction. ....

c) What type of reaction is this? ....

Q4 Esters are commonly used in **perfumes**, **flavourings** and as **solvents**.

a) i) Why are esters used in perfumes? ....

ii) Why isn't it a good idea to take a deep breath when smelling esters?

....

b) Suggest why some people worry about esters being used as food flavourings.

....

c) i) Why are esters used as solvents? ....

ii) Suggest why esters have replaced other organic solvents in things like paint.

....

Electrolysis

Q1   **Complete** and **balance** the following electrode reactions.
For each one, tick the correct box to show whether it is **oxidation** or **reduction**.

	Oxidation	Reduction
a) ....$Cl^- \rightarrow Cl_2$ + ...e^-	☐	☐
b) Ni^{2+} + ...$e^- \rightarrow$	☐	☐
c) ....$O^{2-} \rightarrow O_2$ + ...e^-	☐	☐
d) ....$OH^- \rightarrow$ ....H_2O + O_2 + ...e^-	☐	☐
e) Al^{3+} + ... $\rightarrow Al$	☐	☐

Q2   Electroplating could be used to put a
thin coat of **silver** onto a **nickel** fork.

a)   Complete the diagram by labelling
the **cathode** and **anode**.

b)   What ion must the electrolyte contain?

....

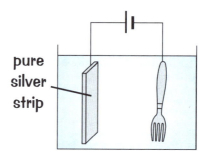

pure
silver
strip

Q3   **Molten copper(II) chloride** is electrolysed using carbon electrodes.

a)   Write the half-equation for the reaction at the **anode**.   ....

b)   Write the half-equation for the reaction at the **cathode**.   ....

c)   Write the full **ionic equation** for the electrolysis of copper(II) chloride.

....

Q4   Study the reactivity series and the table showing the products at the cathodes
when different solutions of **ionic compounds** are electrolysed.

What do you notice about
the substance released at the
cathode and where it's found
in the reactivity series?

....

....

....

....

Ionic Compound Solution	Product at Cathode
sodium nitrate	hydrogen
copper sulphate	copper
sodium iodide	hydrogen
potassium chloride	hydrogen
silver nitrate	silver

reactivity ↑

potassium
sodium
calcium
carbon
zinc
iron
lead
hydrogen
copper
silver

Electrolysis and Cells

Q1 Tick the correct boxes to show whether the following statements are **true** or **false**.

	True	False
a) Copper is extracted from its ore by electrolysis.	☐	☐
b) Copper needs to be very pure for use in electrical conductors.	☐	☐
c) Batteries are electrochemical cells used to produce electricity.	☐	☐
d) In electrolysis, electricity causes a chemical change.	☐	☐

Q2 Copper is **purified** by electrolysis.

a) Draw a labelled diagram in the box provided to show the electrolysis cell used in the purification of copper.

b) Write half-equations for the reactions at each electrode.

Cathode: ....

Anode: ....

c) Explain why pure copper ends up at the **cathode**.

....

....

Q3 The diagram shows an **electrochemical cell**. Zinc is **more reactive** than iron.

a) **i)** Describe what is happening at the zinc strip.

....

....

....

ii) Write a half-equation for this reaction. ....

b) **i)** Bubbles of gas are produced on the iron strip, but the iron strip does not change in appearance or mass. Describe what is happening here.

....

....

ii) Write a half-equation for this reaction. ....

c) Describe how this cell produces an electric current.

....

....

The Alkali Metals

Q1 Join the different **sodium compounds** to their **uses**.

bleach

purification of aluminium ore

soaps and detergents

making ceramics

sodium carbonate

sodium hydroxide

making glass

paper manufacture

fibres

soda crystals

Q2 Complete the passage by choosing from the words below.

molten	Li_2CO_3	alkali	limewater	3500
transition	limestone	Na_2CO_3	coloured	solid 1500

To make glass, a mixture containing sand (SiO_2), sodium carbonate (..........................)

and .... ($CaCO_3$) is heated to .... °C. At this stage,

.... metal compounds can be added to the .... glass to

make it .... As it cools down, the glass turns ....

Q3 Susan's teacher put a piece of **potassium** into a beaker of water containing **universal indicator**.

a) Describe what Susan should expect to see. ....
....

b) Write a balanced symbol equation for the reaction, including state symbols.

....

Q4 The table shows the **melting points** of some Group I metals.

a) What is unusual about the melting points of these metals?

....

b) Describe the trend in the melting point as you move down this group.

....

Element	MELTING PT (°C)
Li	181
Na	98
K	63
Rb	39
Cs	28

c) Complete the following sentences which describe other trends seen in the Group I elements:

i) As you move down Group I, the **size** of the atoms ....

ii) As you move down Group I, the alkali metals become .... to cut.

iii) As you move down Group I, the **reactivity** ....

Sulphuric Acid

Q1   The Contact process is used to manufacture sulphuric acid.
Complete the table to show the **conditions** used in the Contact process.

Temperature:	
Pressure:	
Catalyst:	

Q2   **Complete** and **balance** the following equations involved in the Contact process.

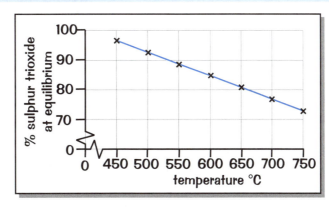

a)   .... + ... → SO_2

b)   .... + ... ⇌ ....SO_3

c) SO_3 + ... → ....

d)   .... + ... → ....H_2SO_4

Q3   The graph shows the effect of **temperature** on the production of **sulphur trioxide**.

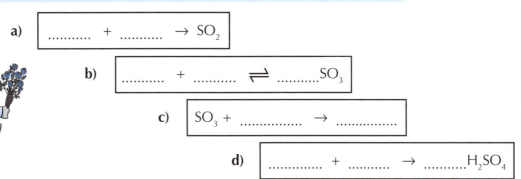

a)   Describe how the percentage of sulphur trioxide at equilibrium changes with temperature.

....

b)   At what temperature would you get 85% sulphur trioxide at equilibrium? ....

c)   What percentage of sulphur trioxide would you get at equilibrium at 750 °C? ....

d)   Explain why it is important to keep the pressure constant when investigating the effect of
temperature on percentage yield.

....

Sulphuric Acid

Q4   Complete the following sentences by circling the correct word from each pair.

> The **reduction** / **oxidation** of sulphur dioxide to sulphur trioxide is **exothermic** / **endothermic**.
>
> When the temperature is increased, you get **more** / **less** sulphur trioxide.
>
> If the temperature of any reaction is increased, the rate of the reaction **decreases** / **increases** because the particles have **more** / **less** energy.
>
> A high temperature gives a **high** / **low** yield of sulphur dioxide, but produces it **slowly** / **quickly**.

Q5   Modern industry uses thousands of tonnes of **sulphuric acid** per day.

a)   The pie chart shows the major uses of sulphuric acid.
What is the **main use** of sulphuric acid?

....

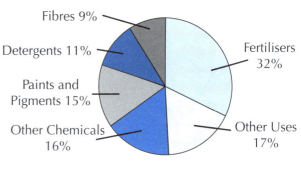

Fibres 9%
Detergents 11%
Paints and Pigments 15%
Other Chemicals 16%
Fertilisers 32%
Other Uses 17%

b)   Give two uses of sulphuric acid in the car manufacturing industry.

1. ....

2. ....

c)   Which of the following compounds found in fertilisers is manufactured from sulphuric acid?

ammonium nitrate   **ammonium sulphate**   **ammonium phosphate**   **potassium nitrate**

d)   Describe how sulphuric acid is used in the preparation of metal surfaces.

....

....

Q6   As part of the Contact process, SO_2 is oxidised to form SO_3 at a pressure of **1-2 atmospheres**.

a)   Explain what would happen to the yield of SO_3 if the pressure was increased.

....

....

b)   Give two reasons why this oxidation is not done at a high pressure.

1. ....

2. ....

Top Tips: Concentrated sulphuric acid causes severe burns. So workers using it in all those industries in Q5 (it's really **economically important**) have to be very careful when handling it.

Detergents

Q1 Many modern detergents used for washing clothes are 'biological'.

a) What is the difference between biological and non-biological detergents?

....

b) Why do biological detergents become less effective at temperatures above 40 °C?

....

c) Circle the types of stain below that biological detergents would clean particularly effectively.

paint   *blood*   *grass*   *tomato ketchup*   *engine oil*

Q2 Fill in the blanks using the appropriate words below.

lowering	miscible	hydrophobic	immiscible
hydrophilic	lift	grease	sugar	raising

Oil and ....-based stains are .... with

water. Surfactants help them to mix with water, by attaching to the fat

molecules in the stain and by .... the surface tension of the

water. The movement of the water in the washing machine helps the surfactant

molecules to .... away droplets of oil into the water.

Q3 The diagram shows a **surfactant molecule**.

a) Complete the diagram by labelling the **hydrophilic** and **hydrophobic** sections of the molecule.

....

b) Which section of the molecule is attracted to:

i) water molecules? .... ii) grease and oil? ....

Q4 Surfactants are made when **fatty acids** react with **alkalis**.

a) Complete the following general equation. **acid** + **alkali** → .... + ...

b) Suggest a suitable alkali to react with fatty acids to make soap. ....

c) What name is given to this neutralisation reaction? ....

Detergents

Q5 Felicity works for a chemical company that is developing a new washing powder. She tests five different powders and records their cleaning effectiveness at different temperatures and against a range of different stains. She uses a scale of 1 (poor) to 10 (excellent).

a) Which powder is best at cleaning grass stains at 40 °C?

....

b) Which powders could be biological detergents? Give a reason for your answer.

....

....

....

		Washing powder				
		A	B	C	D	E
Effectiveness	**at 40 °C**	9	3	5	7	7
	at 60 °C	3	3	9	8	4
	Against tomato stains (at 40 °C)	8	1	5	4	10
	Against grass stains (at 40 °C)	8	4	5	7	3

Q6 In an experiment to investigate the **causes** of **hardness** in water, soap solution was added to different solutions. 'Five-drop portions' were added until a sustainable lather was formed.

Solution	Drops of soap solution needed to produce a lather	Observations on adding soap solution	Drops of detergent solution needed to produce a lather
distilled water	5	no scum	5
magnesium sulfate solution	35	scum formed	5
calcium chloride solution	30	scum formed	5
sodium chloride solution	5	no scum	5

a) **i)** Which ions caused hardness in the water?

....

ii) Explain how you know. ....

....

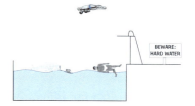

BEWARE:
HARD WATER

b) What role did the test using distilled water play in the experiment?

....

c) Suggest two advantages of using detergent solution rather than soap for washing.

....

d) Explain why scum forms when soaps are added to hard water.

....

e) Explain why water softeners are added to modern detergents.

....

Chemistry in Real Life

Q1 a)   Match the following list of chemicals to the products that they are used to make.

sodium hydroxide

copper compounds

ethanol

sodium carbonate

aftershaves and perfumes

glass

soaps and detergents

dyes and pigments

b)   For all of the chemicals listed above, give a potential danger associated with their general use.

i)   sodium hydroxide ....

ii)   copper compounds ....

iii) ethanol ....

iv) sodium carbonate ....

Q2   Use the information in the table to choose the **best** metal for the following applications.
In each case explain why you think the metal is the best for that application.

Metal	Electrical Conductivity	Thermal Conductivity	Tensile Strength	Reaction with Water	Density (g/cm^3)	Relative Cost
Steel	good	good	excellent	slow	7.8	cheap
Copper	excellent	excellent	good	none	9.0	very expensive
Aluminium	very good	very good	very good	none	2.7	expensive

a)   The wires in electric cables.

....

b)   Girders for building bridges.

....

c)   Plating for the bottom of high-quality saucepans.

....

d)   Lightweight parts for aircraft.

....

Top Tips: Finally, some real-life examples where your expert knowledge might come in handy. Have a flick back if you need some reminders about the chemicals you've come across.

Chemistry in Real Life

Q3 Martha has been asked to produce a new **washing-up liquid**. This new product needs to be good at **removing dirt and grease** in both hard and soft water, and it needs to be able to have a range of **'fruity' smells** such as apple or lemon.

  a)   **i)**   What active ingredient will Martha use in the liquid to remove grease and dirt?

....

        ii)   Describe how this active ingredient can be manufactured.

....

        iii)   Give a safety precaution that will be necessary in the manufacturing process.

....

  b)   **i)**   Martha needs to find a substance to give the washing-up liquids the desired fruity smells. What family of chemicals could she choose from?

....

        ii)   Describe any potential hazards associated with this family of chemicals.

....

Q4 Isobel is developing a new range of **paints** and has asked for advice about the best chemicals to use. Her **product specification** is shown opposite.

> • range of different colours
> • they must be able to paint different materials (such as wood, paper and metals)
> • they must not cost too much to make
> • they must be safe to use
> • they must dry quickly after being applied

  a)   Which group of elements are the coloured compounds in the paints likely to contain?

....

  b)   Suggest three important properties that the company will need to look at when assessing the suitability of different coloured compounds.

....

....

  c)   Two possible solvents for the paints are **water** and **ethanol**. Suggest two advantages and two disadvantages of using ethanol instead of water.

Advantages: ....

Think about how well each solvent matches up with the product specification.

....

Disadvantages: ....

....

Mixed Questions — C3 Topic 4

Q1   An electronics company is investigating metals to make the 'legs' for a new type of **computer chip**. The 'legs' carry **electrical signals** in and out of the chips, as well as **holding** the chip in place. One possible metal for this job is **copper**.

a)   Name **four** properties the metal should have.

....

....

b)   **Copper** can be extracted from its ore by reduction with carbon.
Suggest why copper produced in this way could not be used for making the legs.

....

....

c)   During the purification of copper by electrolysis, what is used as the:

i)   cathode? ....

ii)   electrolyte? ....

Q2   A new **perfume**, 'Back2Basics', is being released. The main ingredients are **water**, **alcohol** and a sweet smelling **ester**.

a)   Give **two** properties of esters that make them well suited for use in perfumes.

....

b)   Explain why the alcohol is present.

....

c)   Another industrial use of alcohol is as a fuel. Give **two** advantages of using alcohol as a fuel.

....

Q3   Iron is a typical **transition metal**.

a)   How is iron used in the Haber process for the production of ammonia?

....

b)   Iron is alloyed with another element to form steel.

i)   Name the other element in steel.

....

ii)   Suggest one reason why iron is used as a structural material.

....

C3 Topic 4 — Chemistry Working for Us

Mixed Questions — C3 Topic 4

Q4 The Paper Street Soap Company make soaps by reacting **esters** with **sodium hydroxide**.

a) The first stage in the process is to produce the ester.
Draw the displayed formula equation for the reaction between propanoic acid and ethanol.

b) During the production process workers in the factory are required to wear masks. Why is this?

....

c) Sodium hydroxide can be produced by reacting sodium with water.

i) Write a balanced symbol equation for the reaction between sodium and water.

....

ii) Sodium is an alkali metal. How does the reactivity of the alkali metals change as you move down the group?

....

iii) Give two properties that make alkali metals unlike other metals.

....

d) The Paper Street Soap Company also produce a range of detergents. Recently the company has received complaints about scum formation from people who live in hard water areas.

i) Why does this problem occur?

....

....

ii) What could the company add to their detergents to reduce this problem?

....

Q5 During the Contact process, **sulphur dioxide** reacts with **oxygen** to form **sulphur trioxide**.

a) Write the balanced symbol equation for this reaction.

....

b) **i)** What are the industrial conditions used during the production of sulphur trioxide?

....

ii) Why are these conditions a compromise? ....

....

CEW41